# Tube Trains on th

## BRIAN HARDY

## Capital Transport

First Published 2003

ISBN 185414 276 3

Published by Capital Transport Publishing
38 Long Elmes, Harrow Weald, Middlesex

*Above* 1928 UCC DM S21S leads a seven-car train in all-blue livery into Brading. *(Geoff Dust)*

*Front cover* Unit 483.007 in London Transport red livery departs Sandown on a northbound working in August 2003, while the end of a dinosaur liveried train can be seen on the left. Unit 483.009 has also been painted red so that a like-liveried four-car train can be formed. *(Capital Transport)*

*Title page* The end of the line and time for reflection. DM 8 of 1931 vintage (ex-LT 3074) is in Fratton on 22 June 1990 after being shipped back from the Isle of Wight on that day. In October 1990, this was one of six cars that returned to Ruislip depot to be stripped of spares for the Heritage Train project, while LT let Network SouthEast have withdrawn Ballast Motor cars of 1938 Tube Stock for Isle of Wight spares. DM 8 eventually went for scrap in January 1993. *(Bob Greenaway, LURS Collection)*

# INTRODUCTION

When any London Underground rolling stock – past or present – is withdrawn from passenger service, its normal fate is the scrapyard. A small few of the more fortunate examples survive in less glamorous roles, usually as engineers' vehicles, while an even smaller number, if they are lucky, survive into preservation. Sometimes, especially in earlier times, Underground cars were sold onwards, to serve as annexes for homes, garden sheds, chicken runs, beach huts, store rooms or even experimental laboratories.

Some of the Metropolitan Railway's steam coaching stock, however, made its way to other operators in the early part of the 20th century, not only in the UK but in northern France as well. Some saw service on the Isle of Wight and several still survive as beach huts at St Helens.

Tube stock was hardly suitable for use on main-line sized railways and the vast majority of it, once withdrawn, never saw revenue earning service again. One exception was that of nine tube coaches of the 1920 Watford Joint Tube Stock which were acquired by the LMS in 1931 for its electric shuttle services between Watford Junction, Croxley Green and Rickmansworth. They worked on these services until the outbreak of the Second World War in 1939, and were then stored and afterwards scrapped.

The further use of withdrawn tube cars was therefore an unlikely event – until replacement rolling stock was being considered for the Isle of Wight in the early 1960s. New trains built to a smaller loading gauge (because of the restricted clearance of Ryde tunnels) was, cost-wise, out of the question. British Railways therefore turned to London Transport for help because at the time, large quantities of Pre-1938 Tube Stock were being withdrawn. The use of this stock was seen as the most practical solution to the problem, and to that end a number of cars once again saw revenue earning service. The same fortune befell a smaller number of 1938 Tube Stock cars when the original trains were long past their sell-by date.

In the following 20 years, there have been extensive changes to the tube stock operating on the Isle of Wight. The original trains provided in 1967 have gone, only to be replaced by more second-hand tube cars working well beyond 'retirement' age.

Part of this work was first published in 1983 by the London Underground Railway Society as issue No.11 of UNDERGROUND, which was an 'occasional' series of booklets about London Underground related subjects. For the updated version, the author would like to express his appreciation to the following, who have helped with advice and information in either or both of the books: Fred Ivey, Laurie Mack, Mike Kennard, Ian Whitlam (Wight Locomotive Society), Allan Barter (Project Manager of the electrification scheme 1966–67), British Rail Southern Region (CM&EE Department) Croydon (first edition) and Alan Hawes (Project Manager of the 1938 Tube Stock 1988–90). Thanks, too, to all those who responded to my request for photographs. The selection process has been long but enjoyable. Many of the photographs in this book come from the late Bob Greenaway's collection, which belongs to the London Underground Railway Society. The map on page 96 is by John Gillham.

The (first) Ryde depot Open Day and the 60th anniversary of rolling stock in January 1984 would not have been possible without the help and support of Max Millard. In addition, thanks are due to Ted Crawforth for making available his comprehensive records, and to the late Les Coote, who was the Manager at Ryde St John's Road depot for some 15 years from the beginning of electric traction on the Isle of Wight in 1967.

Grateful thanks also go to succeeding Depot Managers and staff – Keith Bowden, John Parsons, Mark Brinton, Ian Moone and Andy Snell, along with Jess Harper and the current team – all of whose combined initiatives, dedication and enthusiasm have enabled the ex-London Underground rolling stock on the Isle of Wight to be kept going for so many years. All have been willing to share the information available to me, which has made this book possible – I have always been made most welcome.

Finally, special thanks are expressed to Piers Connor for checking the draft and making many constructive suggestions, and to my wife Jeanne for checking the final typescript.

Brian Hardy
Ickenham, August 2003

## ABBREVIATIONS

### TRAIN MANUFACTURERS

| | |
|---|---|
| BRCW | Birmingham Railway Carriage & Wagon Company Ltd |
| CL | Cammell Laird & Company, Nottingham |
| GRCW | Gloucester Railway Carriage & Wagon Company Ltd |
| MCW | Metropolitan Carriage & Wagon Company Ltd, later Metropolitan Cammell Carriage & Wagon Company Ltd, later still Metropolitan Cammell and today Alstom |
| UCC | Union Construction & Finance Company Ltd, Feltham |

### TYPES OF CAR

| | |
|---|---|
| DM | Driving motor |
| CT | Control trailer |
| T | Trailer |
| NDM | Non driving motor |

### RAILWAY ORGANISATIONS AND EQUIPMENT

| | |
|---|---|
| BR | British Railways (subsequently British Rail) |
| BRML | British Rail Maintenance Limited (Eastleigh) |
| BTH | British Thomson Houston |
| CM&EE | Chief Mechanical & Electrical Engineer |
| DESU | Depot Engineering Support Unit (LUL) |
| DM&EE | Department of Mechanical & Electrical Engineers |
| EMU | Electric Multiple Unit |
| FY&NR | Freshwater, Yarmouth & Newport Railway |
| GEC | General Electric Company |
| HT | High Tension |
| IWCR | Isle of Wight Central Railway |
| IWR | Isle of Wight Railway |
| LB&SCR | London, Brighton & South Coast Railway |
| LMS | London, Midland & Scottish Railway |
| L&SWR | London & South Western Railway |
| LT | London Transport |
| LUL | London Underground Limited |
| MG | Motor Generator |
| NSE | Network SouthEast |
| PCM | Pneumatic Camshaft Mechanism |
| PPP | Public Private Partnership |
| REW | Railway Engineering Workshop (Acton Works, LUL) |
| SR | Southern Region |

# CHAPTER 1
# A BRIEF OVERVIEW

Before the story of the Underground 'tube' rolling stock on the Isle of Wight is told, it would be useful to briefly survey the railway network on the island – how it was built up and how it subsequently declined.

It was in the railway 'mania' age of 1845 that railways for the island were first considered. Opposition to the idea caused early proposals to be abandoned and it was not until 1862 that the first line was opened, having been authorised by an Act of Parliament in August 1859. Subsequently, five separate railway companies operated on the Isle of Wight. The first to commence operation was the Isle of Wight Central Railway between Cowes and Newport on 16 June 1862. The Isle of Wight Railway opened its first section between Ryde (now Ryde St John's Road station) and Shanklin on 23 August 1864, followed by a southern extension to Ventnor on 10 September 1866. The third railway company was the Freshwater, Yarmouth and Newport Railway which first carried passengers on 20 July 1889. The various sections of line to open were:

| Company | Between | Mileage | Total Mileage | Date of opening |
|---------|---------|---------|---------------|-----------------|
| IWCR | Cowes – Newport | 4¼ | 4¼ | 16.06.1862 |
| IWR | Ryde (St John's Road) – Shanklin | 7¼ | 11½ | 23.08.1864 |
| IWR | Shanklin – Ventnor | 4 | 15½ | 10.09.1866 |
| IWCR | Sandown – Shide | 8¼ | 23¾ | 1.02.1875 |
| IWCR | Shide – Pan Lane | ½ | 24¼ | 6.10.1875 |
| IWCR | Smallbrook Junction – Newport | 8 | 32¼ | 20.12.1875 |
| IWCR | Pan Lane – Newport | ½ | 32¾ | 1.06.1879 |
| L&SWR & | (Ryde St John's Road – Ryde Esplanade | ¾ | 33½ | 5.04.1880 |
| LB&SCR | (Ryde Esplanade – Ryde Pier Head | ½ | 34 | 12.07.1880 |
| IWR | Brading – Bembridge | 2¾ | 36¾ | 27.05.1882 |
| FY&NR | Newport – Freshwater | 12 | 48¾ | 20.07.1889 |
| IWCR | Merstone – St Lawrence | 5½ | 54¼ | 20.07.1897 |
| IWCR | St Lawrence – Ventnor West | 1¼ | 55½ | 1.06.1900 |

The total route mileage of the railways on the Isle of Wight amounted to 55½ and was made up as follows:

| | |
|---|---|
| Ryde Pier Head – Ventnor | 12½ |
| Brading – Bembridge | 2¾ |
| Smallbrook Junction – Cowes | 12¼ |
| Newport – Sandown | 9¼ |
| Merstone – Ventnor West | 6¾ |
| Newport – Freshwater | 12 |

From the turn of the 20th century this 55½ route miles of railway was to remain intact for over 50 years. The Isle of Wight, being very much a holiday island, saw heavy passenger traffic in the summer season but during winter months traffic was very light especially on the branches, and the pace was leisurely to say the least. Apart from the Ryde Pier Head to Smallbrook Junction section, which was double-tracked, the rest of the network was single-tracked, with passing loops at some stations. These were at Brading, Sandown, Shanklin, Ashey, Whippingham, Whitwell, Ningwood, Yarmouth, Carisbrooke and Merstone. Newport was signalled and worked as double track between the North and South signal boxes.

An important inclusion in the early railway history of the Isle of Wight is that of the tramway at Ryde, which eventually plays a part in the Tube Stock story. A horse-drawn service was provided from 29 August 1864 along the length of the pier. It was extended through the streets of Ryde in August 1871 to St John's Road, which was then the terminal railway station, providing a connection between ships from the mainland and the railway network of the Isle of Wight. This tramway extension was short-lived, operating for just nine years.

Ventnor was the southern terminus of the Isle of Wight Railway from Ryde and was closed on 18 April 1966 when the line was cut back to Shanklin. No.19 'Osborne' (scrapped in 1955) is seen at the north end of the station with the tunnel under St Boniface Down in the background. Even in the early days of Underground stock on the Isle of Wight, there was talk of reopening to Ventnor. So far, however, in the intervening 35 years, nothing has come of this. (Colour-Rail)

A scene at Ryde Pier Head with 0-4-4T No.36 'Carisbrooke' in charge of a departing train. At this time there were two island platforms and four platform faces at Ryde Pier Head. *(Colour-Rail/Derek Cross)*

Memories of the Isle of Wight railways have been created by the Isle of Wight Steam Railway. Class A1X 0-6-0T No.W8 'Freshwater' runs round its train at Smallbrook Junction on 8 May 2003. This locomotive returned to British Railways from the Isle of Wight in 1949. *(Brian Hardy)*

The LB&SCR and L&SWR in 1877 jointly obtained an Act of Parliament to build a new pier at Ryde and to extend the railway from its terminus at St John's Road in new tunnels under the streets of Ryde (to avoid numerous level crossings) and along the new pier to the Pier Head. An intermediate station was also to be built at what is now Ryde Esplanade, originally identified as Pier Gate.

Trains began running along the pier in the summer of 1880 and from then the tramway reverted to pier operation only, running parallel to the railway. Steam locomotives replaced horses as the motive power on the tramway in 1881 but horses returned in 1884. In March 1886 the horse tram service was replaced by electric trams, operating on an outside third-rail system, the third rail being located 18 inches above the pier decking.

The railway scene was relatively stable in the first quarter of the 20th century and no significant alterations took place until sometime after the formation of the Southern Railway on 1 January 1923. The merger included the Isle of Wight Railway and the Isle of Wight Central Railway. The Freshwater, Yarmouth & Newport Railway disputed the proposed terms of amalgamation and did not become part of the Southern Railway until 1 August 1923.

New passing loops were installed in 1925 at Wroxall and in 1926 at Haven Street, the latter replacing that at Ashey. In 1927 the single-line section between Brading and Sandown was doubled, and in the same year electric traction was replaced on the Ryde Pier tramway by Drewry petrol railcars. It should also be mentioned here that the tramway came under Southern Railway control in 1924. The present signalbox at Ryde St John's Road was originally located at Waterloo Junction in London, but was made redundant and transferred to its present location when the lines into Charing Cross and Cannon Street were electrified in 1926.

The working of the double-track section south of Ryde St John's Road was very interesting. Up to 1926, it was worked as two independent single lines, with the Ventnor trains using the eastern track and the Newport/Cowes trains using the western track. In 1926 a junction and signalbox were installed at the point of divergence of the two routes – Smallbrook Junction. From then until the closure of the Cowes line in 1966 the line from Ryde St John's Road to Smallbrook Junction was worked as a normal double-tracked railway during the summer, but during the winter it reverted to the previous arrangement (with the signal arms removed), thus obviating the need for a signalman at Smallbrook Junction during the winter.

The period after the Second World War saw the obliteration of many thousands of miles of Britain's railways. The Isle of Wight did not escape this and the 55½ route miles was reduced to 25½ in the period 1952–1956. First to go was Merstone to Ventnor West on 15 September 1952, followed a year later on 21 September 1953 by Newport to Freshwater and Brading to Bembridge. From 6 February 1956 the Newport to Sandown route was closed, leaving just two routes – one to Ventnor and one to Cowes – both originating from Ryde.

The various sections of line to close were:

| Between | Mileage | Remaining Mileage 55½ | Closure Date |
|---|---|---|---|
| Merstone – Ventnor West | 6¾ | 48¾ | 15.09.1952 |
| Newport – Freshwater | 12 | 36¾ | 21.09.1953 |
| Brading – Bembridge | 2¾ | 34 | 21.09.1953 |
| Newport – Sandown | 9¼ | 24¾ | 6.02.1956 |
| Smallbrook Junction – Cowes | 12¼ | 12½ | 21.02.1966 |
| Shanklin – Ventnor | 4 | 8½ | 18.04.1966 |

It is these remaining 8½ route miles on the Isle of Wight that interest us for the purpose of this book.

# CHAPTER 2
# PRE-1938 TUBE STOCK

By the early 1960s the fortunes of railways in Britain had altered considerably, usually to their detriment. But for the good luck of a political change, all the remaining 24¾ route miles on the Isle of Wight (Ryde – Ventnor and Cowes) would have closed if Dr Beeching's proposals had been carried through, except perhaps for the heavily-used 1¼-mile section between Ryde Pier Head and Ryde St John's Road. However, before the closure proposals were announced, British Railways Southern Region were already concerned about the condition of the existing coaching stock and the problem of continued steam operation on the island, for much of it dated back to the First World War and even earlier.

The locomotives had originated on the L&SWR, and the coaches mainly with the SE&CR and the LB&SCR. They were of smaller loading gauge than normal, necessitated by the restricted clearance of the tunnels at Ryde, which reduced the height of the island railway cross-section by 10 inches compared with that of the main line railways. Any replacement rolling stock would have to meet this requirement, thus standard size EMUs or DMUs were out of the question, unless very expensive alterations were to be made to the structure and profile of Ryde tunnels. Furthermore, there was no way that the economics of the island's railways could justify a special build of rolling stock.

The first known traces of London Transport involvement with the Isle of Wight dates back to 24 October 1961, when what it is believed the first letter was sent from the then Southern Region to London Transport's Chief Mechanical Engineer. In this letter it was stated that the Isle of Wight coaching stock was of 'considerable antiquity' and shortly needed replacement. The SR, at this stage, were considering using 65 Underground tube trailer cars, forming them into block train sets and operating them with push-pull power cars used as locomotives. (The BR class 73 electro-diesels were a development of a proposal for an IoW motor luggage van). A favourable reply was sent back from LT to the SR saying that investigations would be made into which cars were available and would be suitable.

The tube cars had become available by the introduction of the 1959/62 Tube Stocks onto the Piccadilly and Central lines. Much 'surface' stock was also being disposed of by London Transport (locomotive-hauled and T stock EMU compartment stock coaches, and F stock) but these had to be discounted because of the gauge restrictions.

The Pre-1938 Tube Stock scrapping programme was then in full swing. It began in June 1960 and mostly involved, to start with, the older GEC-equipped stock. Despite the GEC equipment having been renovated, the failure rates on the Underground suggested its earliest replacement in the scrapping programme. The BTH equipment on the 1927–34 cars was deemed more reliable. They outlasted the GEC cars and were therefore available for the Isle of Wight.

Richard Beeching had succeeded Sir Brian Robertson as Chairman of the British Transport Commission on 31 May 1960. He set about preparing a plan for the future of Britain's rail network and on 25 March 1963 the infamous 'Beeching Report' was published. Much of it was taken up with the proposed closure of many unprofitable rail lines – the ultimate goal being a railway system half the size of what it then was.

Whilst many people have viewed Britain's rail closures a result of Dr Beeching's actions in the light of the report, an alternative view, rarely offered, is that it was just a 'report' and the government of the day were free to act upon it or ignore it as they saw fit. As most of the closures took place in the 1964–70 period during Harold Wilson's Labour government, it could justifiably be argued that the rail closures should be laid at the door of his Minister of Transport, who had to approve the closures in the first place. Meanwhile, Dr Beeching was replaced on 31 May 1965 by Stanley Raymond, Dr Beeching having been considered to have done his job.

Insofar as the Isle of Wight was concerned, the Beeching Report recommended that all but the 1¼-mile section between Ryde Pier Head and Ryde St John's Road be closed. Contact between BR and LT thus reduced somewhat to await the outcome of the various public inquiries into the proposed closures. The combined factors of needing to replace obsolete rolling stock and Dr Beeching's desire to close almost all of the remaining lines on the Isle of Wight, saw British Railways begin making plans for closure, which was programmed to take effect in October 1964.

Correspondence with London Transport was resumed in October 1963, when BR stated that proposals to use tube stock were now 'likely' rather than being just a talking point, if only for the 1¼-mile section in Ryde and requested that two tube stock driving motor cars and four trailers be made available. LT said they were prepared to sell DM cars at £280 each, without traction motors, and trailers at £120 each. If necessary, LT would store the cars for the Southern, but would charge additionally for this.

By December 1963 the Southern had re-introduced the proposal to use diesel traction on the island. Two suggestions were proposed. One was to convert the trains to diesel-electric multiple units (DEMU) by installing a diesel generator with a minimum of control gear in each of the driving motor cars. One or two traction motors would be required for each of these cars, and prices were requested from London Transport, who stated that they would sell motors for £75 each. The second alternative was diesel mechanical transmission and tentative agreements were made with the Southern Vectis Bus Company that they would maintain the engines, provided that they were the same Gardiner engines as those then used in their buses.

By 1 May 1964 six Underground cars were earmarked for the Southern Region. Being of the 1931/34 type, these were 3253, 3706, 7166, 7167, 7173 and 7189. LT's numbering system was that Pre-1938 Tube Stock driving motor cars were numbered 3xxx, trailers 7xxx and control trailers 5xxx. Because they were not reversible, they were divided into 'A' and 'D' cars. On the Isle of Wight 'A' cars would have cabs at the Ryde end and 'D' cars would have their cabs at the Shanklin end.

At the end of May 1964, the Southern asked for a total of twelve cars, by which LT assumed four DMs and eight trailers. However, there were not enough trailers available and the SR were promised four 1923 Cammell Laird trailers which would become available in October 1964 from the Northern City Line. By this time the Central and Piccadilly lines had lost all of their Pre-1938 Tube Stock and the best of it was earmarked for transfer to the Northern City Line. On 6 June 1964, a revision to the plans for changing over the Northern City Line stock was made by LT and six DMs and six trailers (all 1931/34) were made available to the Southern Region. In addition to the six cars noted above, the other six were 3074, 3141, 3702, 3703, 7159 and 7181.

The Southern had said that they would be interested in some control trailers from the Northern City Line which they were told would also become available in October. The 61 cars available on the Northern City Line were in relatively good condition, because of the light duty working and tunnel conditions on that line, but the 1923–30 cars were to be replaced by those of 1931-34 origin from the Piccadilly Line.

While it was realised that the older cars were in as good, if not better condition than the newer ones, facilities for coupling and uncoupling trains on the Northern City Line were to be lost with the closure of the line from Drayton Park to Finsbury

Park. This was to facilitate Victoria Line construction work at Finsbury Park which was where most coupling and uncoupling operations were carried out. With this being the case, permanently coupled four-car sets of identical 1931/34 stock were chosen to work the line instead of two- or six-car formations of the older stock.

Meanwhile, the public inquiry into the proposed closure of the remaining lines on the Isle of Wight was held in June 1964.

The first 12 tube cars, plus 12 extra traction motors were moved in two trainloads from Ruislip to Wimbledon on Friday 14 August 1964, from where they were taken into the SR depot. All twelve cars were then moved to SR sidings at Micheldever (between Basingstoke and Winchester) on Sunday 16 August 1964 *(see Appendix 1)*. The SR required the sill-plates to be removed because the platforms between East Putney and Wimbledon had no overhang – just a vertical face flush with the platform edge. The negative shoes were to be raised to their maximum working height and the tripcocks cut out. These 12 cars would have provided enough rolling stock for the section Ryde Pier Head to Ryde St John's Road with the remainder of the network closed. If this had come into being (fortunately it did not), a new bus interchange complex was planned for St John's Road.

In October 1964 the SR stated that they were still awaiting a decision from the Minister of Transport about the future of the island's railways but were assuming that the Ryde to Shanklin section would stay open. This turned out to be good foresight but, while this was still speculation, they estimated that one four-car and five seven-car sets would be required, the four-car being spare. Eleven further DMs and 16 trailers would be required in addition to the 12 cars already purchased and in store at Micheldever.

If the option of locomotive-hauled trains instead of DMU operation was to be exercised, 23 trailers and 23 control trailers would be required instead. Some of these cars would be converted from driving motors, with the equipment compartments being

The north end of Shanklin station in the summer of 1966 with No.W16 'Ventnor', and before the arrival of conductor rails. *(Rob Sheen)*

used as luggage space. The possibility was also considered that all the remaining railway network on the Isle of Wight might be allowed to stay open, in which case the requirement would be for 27 DMs and 34 trailers, in addition to the 12 already purchased. With this in mind, LT agreed to hold all cars displaced from the Northern City Line in October 1964, but would charge the SR for storage on LT metals, as they would be occupying space required for other purposes, and for provision of a regular patrol to prevent damage by trespassers.

By January 1965 LT stated that there were 61 cars available at Ruislip – 22 DMs, 18 trailers and 21 CTs *(Appendix 2)*. All DM cars had the shoegear removed to reduce the risk of traction current earths in Ruislip depot yard and LT agreed to check the cars daily and to water-wash fortnightly. The DMs were of 1927–29 vintage and had BTH equipment (the GEC DMs on the Northern City Line had been replaced during 1963), control trailers 1924–25 and trailers 1923 vintage. There were, however, two control trailers and one trailer of 1927–28 origin.

A start was made in April 1965 in preparing for the transfer of the above cars from Ruislip to Micheldever. BR match wagons E312081 and B498101, which were previously used on tube stock scrap trains, were taken from West Ruislip to Wimbledon Park via BR on 28 April 1965 and plans were made to start moving the cars from May. On each occasion, two formations of four cars between pilots were to be formed.

All cars destined for the Southern were to have their sill plates removed for the reason given earlier, but this was not always done, much to the Southern's consternation. In addition all shoegear was to be removed and tripcocks latched up. Such moves would leave Ealing Common Depot at 20.10 and 20.50 for Wimbledon.

So that the cars could be taken from Wimbledon to Micheldever by a BRC&W Type 3 (D65xx, latterly class 33) diesel locomotive, one of the match wagons was modified with a Westinghouse air pipe. This would ensure that the eight tube cars would have operative brakes while travelling on the Southern. It was necessary to shunt some of the existing twelve cars at Micheldever to accommodate the others.

On arrival at Wimbledon Park it was proposed that the leading pilot car would uncouple and shunt forward, while the rear pilot would just uncouple. A Southern Region sleet unit and match wagon would then come from Wimbledon depot and couple to the tube cars, taking them straight into the depot. The two pilots would then couple together and return to Ealing Common depot via Wimbledon.

In the mid-1960s the District Line had a 20-minute evening service to Wimbledon and it was expected that the stock transfer could be achieved without delaying the service. However, when it was tried for the first time on 14 May 1965, the District service was delayed by the IoW cars' shunting operation and so an alternative scheme was used subsequently as follows. The transfer train went to Wimbledon station where it was shunted, so that the pilot cars were coupled 'back to back' at the east end of the train. The train then proceeded to Wimbledon Park (eastbound) platform, where the LT pilots uncoupled from the remainder of the train. The Southern Region unit and match wagon then came out of the depot, coupled to the tube cars and took them back into the SR depot, the tube pilots returning to Ealing Common.

The second batch of eight cars, in two separate trains, were transferred on 1 June 1965, by which time the Southern had purchased all 61 ex-Northern City cars which had been at Ruislip since October 1964. It was proposed that 24 cars would be transferred on 9 and 23 July and on 6 August. In the event, only 16 more were moved *(Appendix 3)*. The rest could not be made up because the Ward couplers from some of these cars had been removed for further use on engineers' vehicles. To partly overcome the situation, eight Ward couplers from already scrapped Q stock were obtained from the scrap dealer, Cashmore's of Great Bridge. The couplers, being of the type used on surface stock, had to be modified before being used on tube stock, and this work was done at Acton. Thus, at 1 August 1965, there were still 29 SR-owned tube cars at Ruislip Depot *(Appendix 4)*.

In the meantime, in the summer of 1965, the Minister of Transport announced that the line to Newport and Cowes and the Shanklin to Ventnor section should be closed as recommended, but, as anticipated by the SR in October 1964, the Ryde to Shanklin section should remain open as it carried the bulk of the island's holiday traffic. But perhaps the greatest surprise of all to both LT and the SR was that the Minister announced that this section should also be modernised. British Railways itself favoured diesel traction, while local authorities supported electrification. The former pressed for the retention of the Shanklin – Ventnor section, but this was rejected by the Minister of Transport, who was by then Barbara Castle. With hindsight, however, had today's criteria been used in 1965, it is unlikely that the Cowes and Ventnor routes would have been closed. Also in that year, "for marketing purposes", British Railways had been retitled 'British Rail'.

In October 1965 the Southern decided, as a result of the Minister's announcement, that the line between Ryde and Shanklin would be electrified and operated with 46 of the tube cars set aside for them. The decision to convert the tube cars to diesel operation was discarded as the cars would be expected only to last a short while (which turned out not to be the case).

Although costs for diesel traction and electrification were very similar, the question of motive power provision would arise again relatively quickly when the stock became due for replacement. With electrification, when the cars needed replacement, there would likely be further tube stock available. David McKenna, the General Manager of British Rail at the time, determined that the Isle of Wight and Bournemouth line stocks should be converted and refurbished for a short life span of up to ten years. With the Isle of Wight trains, they would later be replaced with 1938 Tube Stock and the Bournemouth line with new stock. In the event, both of these renewals occurred some 12 years late.

The Southern Region confirmed at the beginning of November 1965 that the British Railways Board had approved the electrification scheme and the use of 46 tube cars. In opting for electric traction with the old vehicles, the whole question of the condition of the control gear and cabling came under review. It turned out that the cars needed re-cabling and also minor alterations to equipment, as an earthed negative would be used instead of a fourth rail negative. The total cost allowed for the modernisation project was £½-million.

Much of this was to be spent on altering Ryde Pier Head station, reducing the number of tracks to two with three platform faces and raising the permanent way at other stations along the line to eliminate a big step between train and platform. At Ryde Esplanade, however, the track was to be left untouched, but the platforms had to be lowered at the insistence of the Minister of Transport. Through Ryde tunnel the track and drainage was to be renewed, with the track raised. Track simplification was to take place at other locations.

Third rail electrification at 630V d.c. was chosen and new substations were to be built at Ryde St John's Road, Rowborough (about one mile on the Ryde side of Brading) and Sandown. Electricity was to be obtained from the South Eastern Electricity Board at 33kV. The electrical control room was located at Ryde but subsequently became Havant on the mainland, operation being by land line telephone. Since 1996, the electrical control room has been at Eastleigh.

In December 1965 the Southern Region issued plans for the new daily service, anticipated to commence by Easter 1967. For the winter, two four-car units would be required, four seven-car trains on summer Mondays to Fridays and six seven-car trains on summer Saturdays. One four-car set, to be kept as a spare, was also envisaged. At this stage, the Southern proposed to keep the Pre-1938 Tube Stock only until the 1938 Tube Stock became available some five years later. The total requirement at that time is shown at the top of the next page.

| Requirement | Already on SR |
|---|---|
| 7 'A' DM | 8 'A' DM (3x1931/34, 5x1927/28) |
| 13 'D' DM | 10 'D' DM (3x1931/34, 7x1927/28) |
| 10 'A' CT | 7 'A' CT (7x1924/25/27) |
| 16 Trailers | 15 Trailers (6x1931, 9x1923) + 4 'D' CT (4x1925) |
| 46 cars | 44 cars |

As can be seen from the above table, the numbers of each type of car already on the Southern were not quite what was required. Three of the ten 'A' control trailers required were intended to be used as trailers and their places were taken by three of the four surplus 'D' control trailers. The fourth one took the place of the 16th trailer required. Although this now meant that the Southern was only two vehicles short of its total number of cars, it had one 'A' DM too many, and three 'D' DMs too few at Micheldever. Over the next few months various changes were made which ultimately sorted this out.

The condition of the additional 29 SR cars stored at Ruislip depot was reported upon by LT to the SR in January 1966, 12 of them having defects as follows:

| | |
|---|---|
| Cab door dented and pitted: | 3010 |
| Rusting panels and guttering: | 3009 3045 3288 3315 |
| | 5262 5273 5277 5281 5285 5289 |
| | 7298 |

The other 17 cars were said to be in reasonable condition, with no apparent defects, and were:

| | | | | | | | |
|---|---|---|---|---|---|---|---|
| 3040 | 3041 | 3062 | 3064 | 3313 | | | |
| 5270 | 5287 | 5294 | 5412† | | | | |
| 7029* | 7276 | 7277 | 7279 | 7281 | 7290 | 7295* | 7296 |

* Cars fitted with roller bearing axle boxes.
† Previous number 5012 – it had been renumbered in 1961 to avoid duplication with LT's new A60 stock.

The cost of rehabilitating 46 cars was estimated by LT to be £90,000. This included 20 motor cars at £2,850 each and 26 trailers at £1,250 each, but was in addition to the £14,860 that would be paid for the cars at scrap prices.

At this point, the Southern decided that out of the 44 cars at Micheldever and 29 still at Ruislip, 27 could now be scrapped, leaving the necessary 46 for refurbishment and subsequent use on the Isle of Wight. They were also in favour of one-person-operation of the trains on the island, and approached LT for estimates of the cost of putting door controls in the driving motor car cabs. This was put at £1,000 per cab, but soon fell out of favour because the top of the cab doors were at gutter level and this would cause difficulties for drivers. OPO would only be possible if the cab door tops were extended into the curve of the roof. All this outweighed the estimated savings of one-man operation over the forthcoming years.

In March 1966, ten cars at Micheldever were deemed to be unfit for further use and were rejected. A total of 12 cars were selected from those still at Ruislip which, fortunately, had not been scrapped. These were chosen to replace the ten rejected and also to make up the shortage of two mentioned earlier. At the same time, the balance of 17 ex-Northern City Line cars at Ruislip were also rejected. The situation is summarised in *Appendix 5.*

It is perhaps difficult to understand why six 1923 Cammell Laird trailers were chosen instead of 1931 Gloucester cars, being eight years older. This was because the 1923 cars seated eight extra passengers, had four fewer doors per car to maintain and, having been on the Northern City Line for most of their life, were in good condition. Furthermore, end single doors were undesirable on the severely-curved platform at Ryde Esplanade. To that end, the 1931/34 motor cars were modified so that the end single (guard's) door remained closed when not occupied by the guard.

Meanwhile on the island, those services not saved by the Minister of Transport were withdrawn. These were from Smallbrook Junction to Cowes from 21 February 1966, followed by Shanklin to Ventnor on 18 April 1966. This left just the Ryde to Shanklin section open – 8½ route miles out of the original 55½.

Work started on overhauling and modifying the Underground cars at Acton Works in March 1966, starting with those stored at Ruislip. Charges to the SR for storage of the stock at Ruislip ceased from 31 March 1966. Arrangements had to be made for those cars at Micheldever to be returned and transfers of these 25 cars commenced in May 1966 *(Appendix 6)*.

The work at Acton included overhauling the braking and electrical equipment, and modifying the latter to provide the earth return for operation on the Southern's third rail system. This involved shorting out all the negative fuses, taking off the negative shoebeam and bolting the negative shoelead to the motor frame using the bolt holes which had held the shoebeam. Some cars also had their many layers of paint stripped off down to bare metal, so that the condition of the bodywork could be examined.

In August 1965 London Transport decided that, by the end of the year, they would replace the four-car sets of 1931/34 tube stock on the Northern City Line with 1938 Tube Stock. This was made known to the Southern and an agreement was reached whereby work on the UCC Feltham cars would be deferred so that advantage could

The cars selected for use on the Isle of Wight were repainted at Stewarts Lane depot. On 10 September 1966, DM 3308 built in 1928 by UCC awaits its new Rail Blue livery. The UCC (Feltham) cars were distinguishable from the rest of the Pre-1938 Tube Stock fleet by having a slightly curved section beneath the waist line. *(Bob Greenaway, LURS Collection)*

On the same date, DM S23S (ex-LT 3315) built in 1927 by MCCW is seen in Rail Blue livery awaiting transfer. It was originally proposed that this car would be in unit 044 and to that end was so numbered. It later became part of unit 045. Note that the match wagon, numbered DS1665, is from the Waterloo & City Line. *(Bob Greenaway, LURS Collection)*

be taken of the newer cars. This would also reduce costs as the 1931/34 cars were already re-cabled in Egatube conduit. The Feltham cars on which work had already started, however, were retained. The replacement trains of 1938 Tube Stock for the Northern City Line had been made possible by service reductions in October 1964, not only on the Bakerloo, Northern and Piccadilly lines on which they worked, but right across the Underground network.

In August 1966 the cost of rehabilitation was found to be higher than originally anticipated. Consideration was given to abolishing the four-car spare set to save £9,000, or to run six-car trains instead of seven, saving £8,000. In September, the Southern decided to reduce the stock by three cars and have only one spare DM car. In consequence of this and with the imminence of the 1931/34 cars being available from the Northern City Line, a further ten cars *(Appendix 7)* were rejected, nine from those stored at Micheldever and one at Ruislip. Seven 1931/34 driving motor cars *(Appendix 8)* were selected from the Northern City Line as replacements.

After completion of the electrical work at Acton Works, the cars were transferred to the Southern via Wimbledon between pilot motors *(Appendix 9)*. The first transfer took place on 13 May 1966 and they continued until the last cars left Acton Works on 16 February 1967. At Wimbledon, after detaching the pilot cars, fuses were replaced and the Isle of Wight cars then travelled to Stewarts Lane depot via East Putney under their own power. A small number of cars, stripped of their layers of red paint down to bare steel, were transferred in that condition.

At Stewarts Lane depot the trains were painted in BR blue livery with brown under-frames – they were the first complete BR stock to be painted in this livery – with yellow cab ends on DMs and on control trailers used as such. Control trailers used solely as trailers were given all-blue cab ends. DM cars carried the BR double arrow emblem in white and all had car numbers in white.

Luggage shelves were also fitted, and prototype conversions were carried out at Stewarts Lane on cars 3010 and 7283. In DM cars three longitudinal seats on the east side of the cars were replaced by these shelves and in each trailer and control trailer, two bays of luggage shelves were provided, one on each side, with the loss of six seats. At each luggage rack position, one window had to be panelled over. The interiors were painted in mushroom with white ceilings, but the LT seating moquette was initially kept (the seats having been retrimmed on cars that needed attention) as well as the red and green leather armrests. The moquette on the cars which still had the 'bar-and-circle' design, however, was replaced from the start.

For three-car transfers a four-car unit already transferred was used as a 'pilot'. As these had already been painted in the new livery, the whole formation often comprised cars in blue and red liveries together with some unpainted (bare steel) cars. The SR formed cars into four- and three-car units, classified 4-VEC and 3-TIS respectively, which when coupled into a train became '7-VECTIS', thus reflecting the Roman name for the Island. The 43 cars were numbered as follows:

| | |
|---|---|
| Driving Motor Cars | S1-11, 13, 15, 19–23, 25. |
| Control Trailers | S26, 28, 30, 32, 34, 36. |
| Trailers | S41-49, 92–96 |
| CTs used as trailers | S27, 29, 31, 33 |

Each car number also had an 'S' suffix which normally indicated a vehicle of Southern Railway origin – hardly applicable in this instance, however. The original LT numbers and new BR numbers are listed in *Appendix 10*.

As some cars were transferred to the Southern before the decision was made to reduce stock requirements from 46 to 43 cars, some renumbering took place before the cars entered service with their new owners. S12S (set 043) and S17S (set 036) were renumbered S22S (set 042) and S21S (set 044) respectively, and S23S was reformed from set 044 to set 045. In addition, control trailer S26S (ultimately in set 031) first bore the car number S38S and, with DM S19S (ultimately in set 043), was formed into set 037 (see *Appendix 11* for proposed and actual formations).

Control trailer S38S was, in fact, the first car to arrive on the island, doing so on 1 September 1966. It was coupled to a match wagon and with class O2 0-4-4T loco-motive No.24 'Calbourne', worked to demonstrate for the Minister of Transport the difference in height from platform to car floor level. For this, a pair of passenger doors had to be made operative and this was achieved by connecting an air pipe to the loco-motive and using the outside door 'butterfly' cock. The train ran between Ryde and Shanklin on Sunday 4 September 1966.

Units completed at Stewarts Lane were worked on the SR main line for trials between Wimbledon and Woking, later being based at Fratton for crew training between there and Haslemere. From Fratton, cars were loaded on to a Pickfords low loader by two cranes (one steam, one diesel) until a special rail loading ramp was ready and then carried on the Portsmouth to Fishbourne car ferry, which could only be done when the weather and tides were favourable.

As the driving motor cars were much heavier than the trailers, two Pickfords trac-tors were required for loading on and unloading off the ferry and a special 'bridge' had to be used to avoid placing excessive weight on the ship's drawbridge. Thus dri-ving motor cars had to be transferred on special trips on a rising tide, whereas trailers were transferred on 'service' ships. This was one of the rare occasions where a tide timetable affected the operation of rail vehicles.

Despite extensive researches and appeals for information, the exact transfer dates for all of the cars has never been established, although it is reasonably certain that 15 had arrived on the island by the end of 1965, with many being stored on the 'up' line near Ryde St John's Road. Whilst a timetable was drawn up for the shipping of the cars, any adverse weather or operating difficulties would cause this to be changed.

At Ryde St John's Road depot, the cars were unloaded on to a special ramp constructed in the yard. Here the cars were shunted by the remaining operational class O2 steam locomotives into the correct formations.

Three cars were damaged during transfer to the Isle of Wight. 1923 Cammell Laird trailers S46S and S49S were both damaged during the unloading of the former, which was the only car finally selected to have roller bearing axle-boxes. S46S moved down the ramp at Ryde St John's Road before the winches could be attached and rolled down colliding with S49S. Damage was sustained by both cars, including broken windows, slight distortion of body sides and damaged drawgear and underframe.

Motor car S22S, while being prepared for shipment at Fratton was struck by a main line vehicle at buffer level. This damaged the receptacle box lids and door pillars and broke cab windows and headlight glasses. The car was taken to the island in damaged condition, where repairs were made to it and the two trailers under guidance from LT staff who were based at Ryde. This was done in the locomotive shed at St John's Road (located on the west side of the station) as the works (on the east side) were closed for reconstruction for the 'new' electric trains. The working conditions here could only be described as primitive – compressed air to test doors, for example, was obtained from a suitably positioned stationary steam locomotive.

A modification made at the last minute to the stock was with the operation of the guard's sliding door on the 1931/34 cars. This was made totally independent from passenger doors – even when the guard's position was unoccupied. On the London Underground, unoccupied guard's positions and their doors on 1931/34 cars could be used by passengers. The 1927 MCW and 1928/29 UCC driving motor cars had hand-operated slam-type guard's doors, which had never been intended for passenger use and were therefore locked when not in use.

The whistles fitted to the trains came from ex-Isle of Wight steam locomotives (with their Caledonian style hooters) on the 'A' end cars, and main line type whistles (sounding like those from former 6-PUL units) on the 'D' end cars. The latter came from the E50xx series locomotives (20) and from 2-HAP units (5). The non-smoking accommodation was in the trailer cars of the 3-TIS units and in the motors and trailers (41-46) of the 4-VEC units.

In preparation for electrification, and with only a Ryde to Shanklin steam train service left after April 1966, the service was cut back to Ryde Esplanade after 17 September 1966 so that work on remodelling Ryde Pier Head station (which actually began in 1964) could continue uninterrupted. Work also started in Ryde tunnel and with only one line available for use and no reversing facilities available at Esplanade station, trains had to be 'topped and tailed', having a steam locomotive at each end between there and St Johns Road. The service was withdrawn completely after 31 December 1966 so that final work on electrification could take place – then set for completion in March 1967. In the interim a replacement bus service was provided.

Apart from the track layout changes at Ryde Pier Head, where the number of tracks were reduced to two with three platform faces, no other substantial changes to layouts were made. The line was double-tracked from Ryde Pier Head to Smallbrook Junction and between Brading and Sandown. Apart from Ryde Pier Head and Ryde St John's Road, each of the stations on the route had two platforms, including the southern terminus at Shanklin, beyond which there was a reversing siding (on the former route to Ventnor) for use during busy times. Signal boxes were retained at Ryde Pier Head, Ryde St John's Road, Brading, Sandown and Shanklin. The workshops at Ryde St John's Road on the 'down' side of the station were adapted to maintain 'tube' trains, while on the 'up' side of the line the old steam shed was closed and subsequently demolished.

Some trains of electric stock already delivered were stored on the down (southbound) line between Ryde St John's Road and Smallbrook Junction. The first trial runs were made in early March 1967 after traction current had been switched on. The

On 21 April 1967, just a month after the beginning of electric traction, a four-car train heads north at the site of Smallbrook Junction bound for Ryde. The formation of the line to Newport and Cowes, which closed in 1966, can clearly be seen on the left of the train. The red disc took the place of an oil tail lamp. *(E.W.J. Crawforth)*

new service commenced on Monday 20 March 1967, when a winter service was being operated and not all the sets entered service on the first day – indeed, not all had reached the island by then but by 20 May 1967 all trains had entered service, including the spare DM *(Appendix 12)*.

While the basic service was hourly during winter and half-hourly in the summer, it was on summer Saturdays that the maximum rolling stock was called for, with six trains providing a 12-minute service throughout the line. This left only one driving motor car spare. The working of six trains at Shanklin required both platforms to be in use, the 'down' for arriving trains and the 'up' for departing trains. Trains proceeding from the down to the up platform shunted beyond the station in the Ventnor direction, for about a train's length or so. When fewer than six trains were running, the up line platform was not normally in use, the down platform being sufficient to deal with all passenger movements. A spare train was often to be found stabled in the up platform, especially during winter months. The signal box at Shanklin was opened only when the two platforms were in use. At other times the 'up' road starter from the down platform (which was worked by electric motor and controlled by Sandown signalbox) was used.

By August 1967, serious consideration was being given to re-opening and electrifying the line to Ventnor and for this the Southern were ideally looking for a further eight cars, one seven-car train and one more spare DM car. At this time, the Pre-1938 Tube Stock available with London Transport was limited and was as follows:

2 x 1931 'A' DMs *
1 x 1931 'A' DM without bogies (the bogies were already on the
    Isle of Wight as spares) *
2 damaged DMs
3 x 1928 UCC DMs, previously at Micheldever
2 x 1923 CL trailers
1 x 1924 CL 'A' CT
3 x 1925 MCW 'D' CTs
32 x 1931 BRCW/GRCW trailers *
6 x 1931 GRCW trailers at Micheldever

All except * had been previously rejected.

1928 UCC-built DM S21S had taken the place of S23S in unit 044 by the time this photograph was taken on 31 December 1966, the last day of steam operation on the island. Until the electric service was ready (on 20 March 1967), buses replaced trains between Ryde and Shanklin. This is a line-up of 15 cars stored on the 'down' (southbound) line south of Ryde St John's Road. *(Bob Greenaway, LURS Collection)*

With no 'D' DMs available, it was proposed to form an extra four-car unit (047) by coupling spare DM S10 to set 036, form two new three-car units (036 and 037) each with one 'A' DM, one 1923 Cammell Laird trailer in the middle and one 'D' control trailer. A spare two-car unit (one 'A' DM and one 'D' CT) would also have been provided. It was also decided that if the 1923 trailers were not in good enough condition, 1931 trailers would be used. The previous problem of having extra doors to maintain and having less seating accommodation, would have been eliminated as the end single doors would have to be sealed or panelled over, because the Minister of Transport banned their use owing to the excessive gap between train and platform on the down line at Ryde Esplanade.

By August 1967, the Isle of Wight Railway was in trouble with heavy rail and wheel flange wear, to such an extent that a 30 mph general speed restriction had to be imposed with 10 mph over all points and crossings. This was caused by the quarter-inch difference in gauge between the LT and BR track systems, the latter being true 4ft 8½ins, LT being 4ft 8¾ins. On the island, check rails were installed similar to LT, but there were initially no wheel flange lubricators. The first 13 were hurriedly installed in that month, the remainder as soon as possible afterwards.

The first tube stock car to arrive on the Isle of Wight was former control trailer S38S which was planned to be part of unit 037. A reduction in stock requirements at the last minute from 46 to 43 cars saw the planned unit 037 disbanded. This car then became S26S in unit 031. *(Electric Railway Society)*

The off-loading of the Underground cars was undertaken in the yard at Ryde St John's Road. Class O2 0-4-4T No.24 'Calbourne' is assisting S38S down the loading ramp on 1 September 1966. *(Author's Collection)*

On Sunday 4 September 1966, steam-hauled S38S ventured out onto the remaining railway, operating a gauging trip between Ryde and Shanklin. The car is seen in the 'down' platform at Ryde St John's Road on that day. This was one of six operational control trailers that were provided (there were four others but these were used purely as trailers), although none were actually used in their own right in a three-car formation until 1988 – just three years before withdrawal! *(Author's Collection)*

On 22 February 1967, reconstruction work is seen being undertaken at Ryde Esplanade station, where the platforms had to be lowered slightly to accommodate the tube cars. Electric services were but a month away from starting. *(E.W.J. Crawforth)*

Initially during the winter months, a seven-car train was stabled in the 'up' platform at Shanklin, to provide space at Ryde depot, where unit 046 (then coupled to 032) is seen. *(Rob Sheen)*

In October 1967 LT offered seven cars for the Southern's proposed Ventnor extension, comprising three 'A' DMs (3082, 3310, 3312 – the last two having been re-numbered by 1965 from 3110 and 3112 to avoid duplication with new 1967 Tube Stock), three 'D' CTs (5273, 5277 and 5285) and one 'A' CT (5270). They were subsequently transferred from Ruislip to Micheldever *(Appendix 13)*. This used up all the available Pre-1938 Tube Stock so the 25 'rejected cars' were sent for scrap from Ruislip in the latter part of 1967 and the 15 still at Micheldever were disposed of in 1968 and 1970 *(Appendix 14)*.

At the end of 1967, DM car S15S (LT 3253) was damaged in a shunting mishap in Ryde Works. It had been placed on blocks on a pit road in the shed for maintenance and another motor car was being shunted outside. This over-ran the entrance doors and ran into S15S, pushing it off the blocks. The driving end landed on the floor, while the trailing end fell on to one of the bogies. The estimated cost of repair was put at £3,600 and the time it would have taken to repair it would have been lengthy – not surprisingly it was recommended not to proceed with this option. Thus the Southern was looking for yet one more car as replacement. All LT could offer was withdrawn car 3271, which itself was damaged, but to a lesser extent than the car it was to replace. The cost for this car was £4,300 (£1,300 for repair, £2,700 for rehabilitation and £300 scrap value). Authority to scrap 3271 had been given on 25 February 1967 but it had remained at Acton for a further year, pending ultimate disposal.

In March 1968 the Southern Region were considering withdrawing the Ryde Pier tramway service, which linked Ryde Pier Head with the Esplanade. With this in mind, estimates for rehabilitation of the seven additional cars were requested. These cars were previously earmarked for the proposed reopening of the Shanklin – Ventnor section, but by this time, what little activity there had been on this had ceased. The cars had already been transferred from Ruislip to Micheldever on 9 July 1968. The estimates were also for the conversion of one 'A' DM to a 'D' DM The costs were:

| | |
|---|---|
| 3 DM cars rehabilitated – | £4,500 each. |
| 4 CT cars rehabilitated – | £1,800 each. |
| Conversion of one DM 'A' to 'D' – | £1,100. |

London Transport stated that the work would take at least eight months, in addition to that on the replacement car.

No doubt the question of finance played an important part on future decisions, as the additional seven cars did not get rehabilitated for the Ventnor extension (which was not authorised) nor as an extra train to replace the pier tramway. Instead, just 3271 was agreed upon to replace damaged car S15S, making do with existing stock, even after the tramway closed.

The Ryde Pier tramway closed on 26 January 1969 and a replacement train service was introduced between Pier Head and Esplanade, using one train shuttling between Pier Head and St John's Road (empty from Esplanade to St John's Road). St John's Road was used for reversal as the old crossover at the south end of Ryde Pier (which was actually immediately north of Ryde Esplanade station) had been removed, having been available only for emergency use anyway. As the shuttle service committed one of the train sets, the main service to and from Shanklin had to be reduced to four trains on summer Saturdays and the frequency reduced from 12- to 15-minute intervals. This rendered the 'up' platform at Shanklin superfluous and it was not used again for passengers, the subway under the track being permanently closed. Nevertheless, the maximum service was still provided over the section that required it most – along Ryde Pier.

At the end of November 1968 the Southern gave authority for the repair, overhaul and refurbishment of 3271 to replace S15S, the bogies and certain other items being reclaimed from the damaged car. They were hoping that LT would be able to complete the work by April 1969 so that the 'new' car would be available for the 1969

The Ryde Pier tramway was operated by Drewry railcars, one on each track, and ran alongside the 'main line trains'. The service was permanently closed on 26 January 1969, traffic being left in hands of the railway. One of the railcars is seen approaching Ryde Esplanade. It is ironic that some 34 years later, the formation for the tramway still stands, although much of it has deteriorated considerably.
*(Author's collection)*

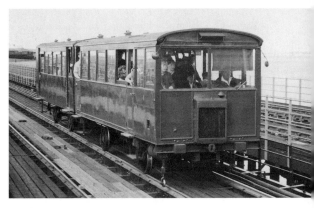

summer service. (It must be remembered that at this time six seven-car trains were operated on summer Saturdays and without S15S or a replacement, there was no spare car at all). Unfortunately, because of staffing difficulties in the repair shop at Acton Works, the immediate repair of 3271 was not possible. In January 1969 an alternative was suggested, in that as four pilot motor cars were about to be withdrawn, one could take the place of 3271. The repair work would be unnecessary and both cost and time reduced, although completion could only be in time for the summer season of 1970. Two MCW cars were offered – 3273 (formerly 3073) built in 1931 and 3707 built in 1934, of which 3273 was found to be in better condition.

Protracted discussions ensued, but at about the time work could have started, there was a three month strike of craftsmen at Acton Works. DM 3273 was chosen as the replacement for the original S15S (3253) on the Isle of Wight and that originally earmarked (3271) was scrapped in November 1969.

After the strike was over, LT had a large backlog of work and hence asked the Southern if they could do the work themselves. This was thought not to be feasible and missing the summer schedules completely, 3273 eventually entered Acton Works on 8 October 1970. The price had increased to £4,330 for overhaul and refurbishment only, plus £200 scrap price for the car body. The bogies and motors from S15S were delivered to Acton during December 1970 and January 1971.

Arrangements were made with Pickfords and the Southern to move the replacement car from Acton direct to the Isle of Wight by road and ship. The previous removal of the loading and unloading ramps at Fratton meant that it was no longer possible to undertake the move partly by rail and partly by road/ship. The transfer was arranged for 20 March 1971 from Acton Works and the following day by ship to the Isle of Wight. A 45ft length of second-hand track was purchased by the Southern from LT at scrap prices, and this was placed on a low loader at Acton.

A seven-car train of Pre-1938 Tube Stock on Ryde Pier heads towards the Pier Head on 24 September 1970. At this time the Pier Head signal box was still open and the train is heading for the left-hand platform, as confirmed by the number '1' under the semaphore arm.
*(Bob Greenaway, LURS Collection)*

25

Because of weight restrictions at Portsmouth and the desire not to use the special 'bridge' again on the ferry, the traction motors were not fitted but returned to Ryde separately by BR lorry. The refurbished car, painted in BR rail blue livery by LT, was transported, complete with its bogies, on the low-loader, which with the track made a total height of 14ft 7ins – only four inches less than the clearance available on the ferry. Also numbered S15S, it entered service for the summer 1971 season, the original car having been scrapped on 10 May 1969.

Excluding the replacement car S15S, a total of 83 cars were initially involved with the Isle of Wight story, which can be summarised as follows:

|  | Cars | Total |
|---|---|---|
| 12 cars to Southern Region August 1964 | 12 | 12 |
| 61 cars available ex-Northern City Line October 1964 | 61 | 73 |
| 7 cars ex-Northern City Line autumn 1966 | 7 | 80 |
| 7 cars ex-Ruislip for proposed Ventnor extension (of which four already ex-Northern City October 1964) | 3 | 83 |
| Total cars for Southern Region | 83 | |
| Less – | | |
| 43 cars to Isle of Wight 1966–67 | 43 | 40 |
| 25 cars scrapped ex-Ruislip 1967 | 25 | 15 |
| 8 cars scrapped ex-Micheldever 1968 | 8 | 7 |
| 7 cars scrapped ex-Micheldever 1970 | 7 | – |

Trialled in 1970 was a change from using 'Osglim' pilot light bulbs to the use of standard fridge-type 15w pygmy bulbs instead. The difference in price was considerable – £2.7s.6d against 6d – 95 of the fridge-type bulbs costing the same as one Osglim! Another early modification was the fitting of a slanting rainstrip over the driver's cab doors on DM cars.

Whereas the painting of the 43-vehicle Isle of Wight fleet was undertaken at Stewarts Lane, the replacement S15S was done at London Transport's Acton Works in early-1971. The replacement car is seen in the Paint shop on 18 February 1971, with the inner end of a 1959 Tube Stock car (left) and repainted COP trailer 014076 on the right. The solebars of S15 are painted blue – they were repainted black before being shipped to the Isle of Wight. (Bob Greenaway, LURS Collection)

The replacement S15S is seen in Acton Works yard on 17 March 1971, by which time the solebars had been painted black. Note that the destination box and train set number bracket in the offside cab window are still in position. (Bob Greenaway, LURS Collection)

The replacement car S15S left Acton Works for the Isle of Wight on 20 March 1967. Its original LT number was 3073 but had become 3273 in 1965 to avoid number duplication with the forthcoming Victoria Line stock. It was ready for service for the summer season in 1971 and is seen in the middle of a seven-car formation at Brading on 17 July. By this time, the train set number bracket had been removed and the destination box painted over. *(Bob Greenaway)*

For the winter of 1971/72, former control trailer S31S, in use as a trailer on the Isle of Wight, was fitted with de-icing equipment. When required to spread de-icing fluid, a member of the staff from Ryde Works operated the equipment from the cab, turning the flow of fluid off while standing in stations. While running, collector shoes detected which side the conductor rail was situated and the fluid applied by operating manual valves appropriately. Indicator lights in the cab showed which side was spraying. One might have considered this costly in manpower, but apparently two round trips in the course of a day were enough to keep the current rails clear in all but the severest of weathers.

The de-icing equipment was installed by enterprising staff at Ryde Works. A report of this 'bargain basement' conversion, which used materials to hand plus £5 for a few additional items, was included in 'Modern Railways' in April 1972 and so came to management's attention. A rebuke was served for not submitting plans and seeking authorisation – though it is believed that the Ryde men were later given a staff suggestion scheme award for their recalcitrant deed!

Another modification made to the trains in the early years was the fitting of straight but slanting rain strips over the side driving cab doors. The exact date cannot be ascertained, but it was soon after 1971.

Ryde Pier Head signal box, perched precariously on the pier on the up line just south of the station, was becoming structurally dangerous and the scissors crossover had become due for renewal. Whilst a specially fabricated replacement crossover existed, the lack of a practical method of lifting in the new components at the seaward end of the pier, and also the cost of sea-proofing the point motors, militated against its installation. So, from October 1973, single line working was instituted over the up line.

The scissors crossover was replaced by plain track and a new crossover installed immediately south of Ryde Esplanade station, giving indirect access to the old down line along the pier which was retained for exclusive use by the pier shuttle service – no longer did it have to run empty to and from Ryde St John's Road to reverse. A pinch-check-rail trap protects any overshooting pier shuttle train from running away down the 1 in 50 gradient towards the tunnel where the double track section then commenced. New colour light signals were installed and the whole area was controlled from Ryde St John's Road signalbox as from May 1974, Ryde Pier Head box being closed and demolished. The pier shuttle train was normally isolated on the east-side track on the pier for its day's turn of duty. The special scissors crossover intended for Ryde Pier Head was subsequently acquired by the Bluebell Railway who incorporated it in their layout at Sheffield Park!

In July 1979 Shanklin signalbox was closed and the disused up platform track and shunting neck beyond Shanklin station were removed. The down platform was extended at the Ryde (north) end and cut back at the Ventnor end, so that the line actually finished on the north side of the bridge across Landguard Road. The bridge was demolished in October 1979. The rationalisation and remodelling of Shanklin was completed by July 1980. The trackbed beyond Shanklin towards Ventnor became largely a woodland walk, although some industrial development has subsequently occurred. This, effectively, prevented any reinstatement of the line to Ventnor, without costly land re-acquisition or probably even more costly route diversions, despite ongoing plans to do so.

DM S8S (ex-LT 3074) leads a seven-car train from Ryde tunnels (the principal reason for tube stock on the Isle of Wight) into Ryde Esplanade on 17 July 1971. Rain strips over the train driver's side cab doors had not at that stage been fitted. *(Bob Greenaway, LURS Collection)*

A contrast in the front ends of the different batches of Pre-1938 Tube Stock at Ryde Esplanade. On the left is a 1931/34 DM car and on the right a 1928/29 UCC DM. Note the difference at the car corners, more angular on the later cars (because they were slightly longer and thus tapered inwards) but with a gentle curve on the older cars. By this time rainstrips had been fitted over the side cab doors, being slightly longer on the newer cars because the cab door was set slightly further back from the corner edge. *(Bob Greenaway, LURS Collection)*

1928 UCC DM S21S of 4-VEC unit 044 is at the south end of a seven-car train awaiting departure from Ryde Pier Head whilst still in all-blue livery, but after the fitting of a rainstrip over the side driving cab doors. The below waist level 'bulge' unique to UCC-built tube cars is evident here. *(Geoff Dust)*

The fleet of 43 cars on the island was reduced over the years because of various mishaps and all are summarised in *Appendices 15 and 16*. However, the fact that cars could be uncoupled individually resulted in numerous temporary and short-lived formations, many of which have gone unrecorded.

Already mentioned was the replacement of S15S in 1971, which then stripped LT of all its available Pre-1938 Tube Stock. On 10 September 1973 a collision occurred at Ryde St John's Road between sets 035 and 045. This led to the withdrawal of three cars (48, 45 and 23) and a good four-car unit was thereby made up from the remaining four cars (6-34-95-9). This in fact comprised one car of 045 and three of 035, and the whole combination was renumbered 045. This left a gap in the three-car unit numbering sequence and 036 was renumbered 035 for unit continuity, but not until 1974.

On 8 September 1975 driving motor S25S from unit 046 was severely damaged by fire at St John's Road depot and was immediately withdrawn from service, being totally beyond repair. The three cars of 046 (8-49-46 – M-T-T) were used as required, coupled to another four-car set, but it was not until October 1980 that it was officially recognised as a three-car unit, taking the erstwhile number 036. As the south end of the unit was a trailer with no cab, it was thus not painted yellow and the set number 036 was displayed in black lettering on a yellow rectangle located at the top of the communicating door.

In 1982 the DM and CT of 033 were withdrawn (the DMs between 033 and 043 having been previously exchanged) – the age of the stock by now starting to take its toll. The DM (S19S) was painted engineer's dark green and had its windows panelled over and was taken to Sandown on 8 March 1984 for use as an equipment store, while the CT (S30S) became used as a store in Ryde depot. The DM was renumbered 08.3569 but the CT remained unchanged.

Therefore in 1982 the fleet comprised 37 cars – five three-car units (031/32/34/35/36) and five four-car sets (041-045), plus a spare DM (S10) and trailer (S93 from set 033). This reduction in stock explains why in 1982 a further reduction was made to the peak summer Saturday service with three trains instead of four, running every 20 minutes instead of 15, plus, of course, a pier shuttle.

All cars were given a new exterior coat of paint in the winter of 1971/72, retaining the all-blue livery. The interiors were repainted during the following winter. From 1976, external repaints emerged from Ryde Works with the passenger doors painted grey, enhancing the plain all-blue appearance of the trains. At the same time the 'S' suffix on car numbering was also dropped. The BR standard blue and green seating moquette was also being introduced at this time, initially being dealt with at Swindon Works but later Ryde Works took over the work. The LT leather armrests were also phased out around the same time. A new interior colour scheme was introduced in late 1981, when lime green and white replaced the drab mushroom and white, the first unit to be done being 032. Perhaps the greatest surprise of all came in early 1982 when exterior repaints saw the introduction of the 'Inter City' blue and grey livery, with black painted cab window surrounds and 'Isle of Wight' lettering on the DM car sides.

From 1969, a system of class numbering for BR EMU rolling stock was introduced. The Isle of Wight sets were classed 451 (3-TIS) and 452 (4-VEC), but a review of BR class numbering in 1973 altered them to become classes 486 and 485 respectively. It was not until the advent of the Inter City livery, however, that these class numbers were first displayed, being placed in the space occupied by the old destination plates. As 'Isle of Wight' letter transfers were not available to start with, S5 ran without these or a BR logo for a while, and S13 and S20 had no BR logos for a short period, but did have Isle of Wight names – hand-painted on. All cars were properly signed by early May 1982. It is interesting to note that all cars had been previously repainted into the 'grey doors' livery before the advent of the blue and grey colour scheme, the last being S29 in October 1980.

The 'grey doors' livery was introduced in 1976 and gave a little colour relief to the original all-blue scheme. Car numbers also omitted the 'S' suffix. In ex-works condition, DM S8 arrives at Sandown on 7 July 1979 heading for Ryde. On the left a train waits clearance for the single line section to Shanklin. Note the 'shunt' signal under the main semaphore arm, provided for trains that terminated at Sandown instead of continuing to Shanklin. *(Bob Greenaway, LURS Collection)*

For the peak summer Saturday service, six seven-car trains were required, giving just one motor car spare. The nominated spare was S10S (ex-LT 3696), a 1934 MCCW DM car, substituting as necessary for cars requiring workshop attention. For this reason the car retained the set number bracket in the offside cab window to display the unit number it was working at the time. However, in this July 1979 view at Shanklin, the unit number displayed on S10 is 035, despite the leading unit actually comprising four cars! For some reason, this car did not have rainstrips fitted over the cab doors until several years after the rest of the DM cars. Note the abandoned track and platform of the former 'up' line on the right. *(Brian Hardy)*

Four-car unit 043 arrives at Ryde Esplanade whilst working the Ryde Pier shuttle service in July 1979. The leading car is 1928 UCC DM S19. The grey doors livery enables the centre door pillar to be easily seen. *(John Herting)*

It was reported on television on 5 July 1982 that the Isle of Wight County Council had approved a grant of £15,000 for internal refurbishing of all the rolling stock on the island. New yellow/orange/brown moquette, as used on LT's 'D' stock would be fitted by summer 1983 and new orange linoleum would be used on the floors, replacing the traditional slatted maple wood.

It seemed that the trains, then varying in age from 49 to almost 60 years, were to go on indefinitely, even though they were originally given a five-year (later ten-year) maximum lease of life when acquired in 1966–67. The new yellow/orange/brown seating moquette was fitted between October 1982 and May 1983, motor cars S9 and S10 being the last. In all, the new moquette was fitted to 37 cars. Seven cars had already been fitted with dark grey or black floor linoleum during 1980–82 but the orange was introduced on an as required basis from December 1982. It was not until December 1988, however, that the 13 outstanding cars were so treated – then as a matter of urgency! In the interim period, some cars had only sections of maple wood floor replaced by linoleum.

The oldest Underground cars on the Isle of Wight were the trailers which were built in 1923 by Cammell Laird. S92 (ex-LT 7285) pauses at Sandown. Note the signalbox on the platform which stood high above the station. *(Brian Hardy)*

The Inter City (!) blue and grey livery was first applied to the Pre-1938 Tube Stock from 1982 and when the original three- and four-car units were abandoned in favour of five-car units, there were many alterations to the train formations. For a time the DM ends had a white figure applied just above sole-bar level (in this case '4') indicating that it would be five-car set 044. DM S7 leads a five-car formation into Brading. Note that the door tread plates have been picked out in red and that the vents above the front cab door have been sealed. (Brian Hardy)

The driving cabs of these trains were considered to be draughty and a programme began in 1985 to seal up the front cab door. The conversion on a DM car is seen in progress in St John's Road workshops. (Brian Hardy)

The end result is depicted here on a five-car train arriving at Ryde St John's Road with DM S6 leading. The surrounds to the cab windows were painted black, which was extended downwards on the offside to present a symmetrical appearance. A black 'Isle of Wight' silhouette was added to the otherwise blank front. (Brian Hardy)

S20 is a 1928 UCC DM and is seen in unmodified form at the north end of a train at Shanklin. *(Brian Hardy)*

At the same location the same DM has assumed the temporary unit number of 032. The front cab door was not removed but was panelled over in January 1988 as a temporary measure until the modifications programme was such that there were sufficient cars to work the normal service. DM S20 was the last of the UCC (Feltham) motor cars (which originally had hand-operated guards' swing doors) on the Isle of Wight. *(Brian Hardy)*

A feature of the Pre-1938 Tube Stock built up to 1928 was that DM cars had centre door pillars between the double doors. By this time much repanelling work had taken place and some of the ventilator scoops on the clerestory had been removed. *(Brian Hardy)*

In 1984 a special event was held on the Isle of Wight, which celebrated 60 years in service of the (then) oldest Underground car in passenger service. This was Cammell Laird trailer S43 (ex-LT 7275). It was formed into unit 042 for the occasion and DM S22 is seen ascending from the tunnels at Ryde into Ryde Esplanade Station on 28 January 1984. S22 was the only 1929 UCC DM on the Isle of Wight. The motor cars on this batch of stock omitted the centre door pillar and had ventilator scoops over the equipment compartment instead of louvres. *(Brian Hardy)*

In 1983, work began on removing the yellow-painted cab ends on control trailers. The driving equipment was also removed from the cabs at the same time, but the area was not opened up for public use, as the similarly treated Central Line control trailer cars on the Underground had been in 1955–58. The former control trailers that had been in use as trailers (having blue-painted cab ends) also had what remained of their equipment removed. This included the removal of the headlight fittings and their external shutters, these positions being panelled over. Control trailer S31 retained its de-icing equipment in the denuded cab, and a pair of lights were fitted at solebar level to illuminate the track when actually undertaking de-icing duties.

In January 1984, British Rail decided to celebrate the anniversary of the oldest tube car in service on the Isle of Wight. This was 1923 Cammell Laird trailer S43 (ex-LT 7275, which had entered service 60 years previously on the Hampstead & City Line – now part of the Northern Line – on 28 January 1924) and had been painted for the occasion in the then new blue and grey livery. In the centre section under the car window was the BR double arrow symbol with '1924' on the left and '1984' on the right. The car was formed into a four-car set (22-93-43-15), all being in the new livery.

The 'special' car S43, however, although repainted as recently as August 1983, was repainted again for the occasion. The motor cars carried headboards in the shape of the London Transport roundel, which were fitted on the tail lamp bracket. Being winter time, the train was able to operate as an additional service for visiting enthusiasts, without interfering with scheduled trains connecting with the mainland ships, or people travelling on timetabled services and not interested in the event. For the first time in its long history, Ryde Works at St John's Road opened its doors to the public. The whole event was arranged and hosted by British Rail, with assistance from the Electric Railway Society, London Underground Railway Society and the Southern Electric Group.

The 60-year-old celebrity stands in the bay platform at Ryde St John's Road, prior to picking up passengers on 28 January 1984, working as an additional train in service for the main part of the day. The car was specially repainted for the occasion with '1924' and '1984' placed either side of the double arrow logo. (Bob Greenaway, LURS Collection)

The modernisation of the Pre-1938 Tube Stock on the Isle of Wight was to continue, as will be told later. However, this was not without some rationalisation of facilities and reduction in rolling stock and services. One of the economies was the closure of Brading signal box and the singling of the line between there and Sandown, extending the area of single line operation from Smallbrook Junction to Sandown. Brading, however, had been a useful point for trains to pass. It had enabled a 30-minute 'clock-face' interval service to be provided at off-peak times (during late evenings and on winter Sundays it was hourly) and still enabled a 15-minute service to be provided at busy times.

With Brading signalbox closed from 28 October 1988 and thus lost as a passing point, the only service that could be provided was in multiples of 20 minutes, with trains passing around Ryde St John's Road and at Sandown. A 20-minute off-peak (and 'busy' service) was indeed provided for a time from 11 May 1987 but the two trains per hour service was later reinstated, but perhaps at the less than satisfactory alternate 20/40-minute interval pattern.

The signal frame from Brading was acquired by the Isle of Wight Steam Railway. Brading station remained lit by gas until October 1986, when electric lighting was introduced – the fittings, however, were in a style sympathetic with the old ones.

Further economies resulted in the signal box at Sandown closing on 25 February 1989 and subsequently being demolished, with signals at what is now a passing loop being automatically controlled but monitored by the signal box at Ryde St John's Road – but for difficulties with commissioning this facility, the signalbox at Sandown would have closed at the same time as Brading. This rather tall and conspicuous signal box was located in the middle of the 'up' platform and towered way above the platform canopies, which were themselves demolished prior to the signalbox closing. From then, the complete 8½-mile line was controlled from the signal box at Ryde St John's Road, with both lever-operated signals and electronic control.

When trailer S43 was repainted for the 60-year event, the step treads were painted red with the lettering picked out in white. Future repaints of other cars were subsequently treated the same way. (Nick Agnew)

On the positive side, two new stations have been provided. The first was at Lake, which opened on 11 May 1987. This comprised a single wooden platform of five-car length (effectively putting an end to seven-car train operation) and was provided at a cost of £80,000 after many years of discussion with the local authority. The second station was opened on 20 July 1991 at Smallbrook Junction. This was provided to enable interchange with the Isle of Wight Steam Railway, whose operating area (Wootton to Haven Street) was extended to Smallbrook Junction from the same time, although the intermediate station of Ashey was not ready until 2 May 1993.

Each operator has a single wooden platform on the south side of the junction which enables public interchange between the two services. However, Smallbrook Junction station is open only when the Steam Railway is in operation, there being no road access to the immediate area. As an aside the Wight Locomotive Society was formed in 1966 and set up its headquarters at Haven Street. It began operating between Wootton and Haven Street in the summer of 1971, but was officially opened in 1975.

Among the options considered by BR in the early 1970s was the replacement of the Pre-1938 Tube Stock by 1938 Tube Stock, the scrapping of which began in 1973. These were then deemed to be unsuitable because of their underfloor-mounted equipment, which would be exposed to the elements on Ryde Pier during bad weather, and because of the expenditure which would be necessary to adapt Ryde Works to give proper access to the underfloor equipment. The former obstacle turned out to be something of a misnomer, for the present trains (see Chapter 4) do not run along the pier in especially bad weather – and neither did the old trains! Consideration was also given to using the 1959/62 Tube Stock but it was then thought that it would be a further ten years (from 1985) before it would become available (which in fact it was).

We must now return to see what happened to the Pre-1938 Tube Stock on the island. A new livery had been introduced in 1982 and the brightening up of the car interiors had begun in 1981. However, further improvements would have to be made if the trains were to survive – the slogan 'the age of the train' was taking on a different meaning from that originally intended!

Traffic offerings resulted in the decision being taken in 1985 to rationalise the fleet further, by reforming the best of the remaining cars into two- and five-car units. Meanwhile, a rewiring programme was under way on car lighting, whereby the lights were removed from the cantrail positions just above the windows and, using existing fittings, relocated along the centre of the ceiling, provided alternately on each side of a cable-carrying metal duct, running from one end of the car to the other. The opportunity was also taken to seal the ventilators over the communicating doors at the car ends. Additional vertical steel poles were fitted to carry the wiring and doubled up as additional grab poles for passengers. At the trailing ends of the driving motor cars, where the lighting conduit would go right to the car end, the centre ceiling pilot light for the guard was removed and a new pair – one on each panel – was fitted. The first car to be rewired was control trailer S31 in December 1984.

Another concern with the old trains was the condition of the driver's cab for drivers – they were draughty and let in water. DM S5 was the first to be rewired and was modified with the vents above the front cab door sealed and the front cab door itself was removed and panelled over, giving a flush front appearance. Inside the cab, some of the equipment switches were relocated, making them more accessible. The work on S5 was completed in June 1985. It was this cab end modification that probably resulted in the DMs looking less than ever like 'Underground' trains – even the blue and grey livery with the 'black eyes' painted around the front cab windows had not detracted from the fact that they were still Underground-looking trains! On modified cars on the yellow front ends, the name 'Ryde Rail' was applied, as was an all-black 'blob' in the shape of the Isle of Wight itself. This was also applied (in white on the blue paintwork) to the car sides. To promote the new 'Ryde Rail' name, another Open Day was held at Ryde Works on 21 June 1986.

Not all cars were to modified as it was decided to reduce the operational fleet further to 32 vehicles, comprising five five-car trains and seven spare cars, which could form one more five-car train and give two spare motor coaches, if required. To that end, the first five-car set ran in service on 6 March 1985 in the formation M-T-T-T-M. Two days prior to that, trials with two-car trains (M-M) were carried out, continuing spasmodically until the end of April 1985. This was in connection with operating short trains in the winter with conductor-guards, reducing the need for ticket offices, where they remained, to be staffed at quiet times.

The five-car formations did not necessarily follow a pattern in relation to previous unit formations but all DMs were taken from the 1931/34 type. While the reformations took place, temporary white numbers '1' to '5' were applied just above solebar level at the corner of the cab ends. Being placed on yellow, the temporary numbers did not show up too well but were sufficient for the job intended – to assist identification for staff in Ryde Works. The seven spare cars were to be utilised to replace other cars having lighting and cab end modifications carried out.

As with all best laid plans, seven-car trains did operate again, two being formed for the summer 1985 season. However, another change of plan resulted in the fleet being reorganised into 5x5-car sets, 2x2-car sets along with four spare trailers (total 33 cars and plus one over the previous plan). The net result was that trailer S95 was reinstated, while the four surplus cars (DMs S13 and S21, CT S36 and trailer S96) were dumped beside the 'up' line at Ryde St John's Road in June 1985 for scrapping, along with S30, used since withdrawal in 1982 as a stores vehicle in Ryde depot.

Although the programme of lighting and cab end modifications (on DM cars) continued, in 1987 it was decided to reduce the fleet by a further six cars, making 27 cars in all, comprising 5x5-car sets and 1x2-car. The six withdrawn cars (DMs S15, S20 and S22 and trailers S41, S42 and S46), plus former S19 used as an engineering store at Sandown, were disposed of in 1989 from the yard at Sandown by a local Isle of Wight scrap dealer. DMs S15 and S20 continued to operate in service until the cab modification programme on the main fleet was complete, finally being withdrawn in April 1988. Because these two cars had cabs that were unmodified and they were still required for service, albeit for a short period of time, the winter conditions of 1987–88 were such that the fronts were panelled over in January 1988 to eliminate the draughts and the wet. The front cab doors, however, remained in situ behind the panelling. DM S20 was the last motor coach of the Feltham type (with centre door pillars and hand-operated guard's doors) to survive on the Isle of Wight.

Three DM cars were not repainted into blue-and-grey livery before acquiring Network SouthEast colours. One of these, S4, is seen in the depot yard at Ryde St John's Road. This car, at least, did receive the 'Isle of Wight' branding like its blue-and-grey counterparts. (*Brian Hardy*)

Becoming part of the Network SouthEast network in 1986, it was not surprising that the stock was painted in the new livery. It did, however, lack the diagonals that were applied to main line stock and sat rather well on the Underground cars. This livery saw car numbers omitting the 'S' prefix. This photograph, taken at Sandown on 2 May 1989 with DM 1 at the rear of the train, shows the signalbox still in situ, although it had been taken out of use on 25 February 1989. It was subsequently demolished. *(Bob Greenaway, LURS Collection)*

The Isle of Wight electric line became part of 'Network SouthEast' and in common with rolling stock on the mainland, a new livery was introduced on the Isle of Wight trains. Early in 1987, repainting of rolling stock resulted in the new Network SouthEast livery being applied to the Pre-1938 Tube Stock. The first train, in the formation 10-93-9, entered service in the new colours on 28 February 1987, the trailer car still retaining its original chains at the ends of the car of 63 years previously, which were provided to stop passengers falling between carriages. (Simple grab handles soon replaced them, but going full circle, dedicated 'inter-car barriers' were installed on all London Underground rolling stock from the end of the 1990s). The Network SouthEast livery was adapted to suit the Pre-1938 Tube Stock, as seen above, and this it did rather well. Cars repainted in this new livery saw the 'S' prefix omitted from the car numbering. By this time, all the remaining former control trailers were being used as trailers. To that end, even the former driving cab ends were painted black, as were the trailing ends on all other cars.

The last operative three-car set of Pre-1938 Tube Stock remained for winter de-icing duties from September 1990 but its last recorded use was on 17 February 1991, by which time the yellow ends were becoming somewhat faded. The last three cars were eventually scrapped in April 1994. *(Bob Greenaway, LURS Collection)*

The final reorganisation of rolling stock on the island resulted in a two-car set being formed, comprising a 'D'-end DM and an 'A'-end CT. Because there were no longer control trailers in their own right on the Isle of Wight (all the equipment had been removed a few years previously and the cars were being used as trailers), driving equipment had to be reinstated in the cab of S28. The replacement control equipment took the space of two seats (reduced from 38 to 36) in the passenger saloon immediately behind the driver and small ventilation louvres were fitted. The original style headlights and their exterior shutters were not, however, reinstated. In their place, a halogen headlight and tail light was fitted, as was a BTH spring type master controller rather than the 'solid' (non-spring) master controller with a 'deadman' button as hitherto. The 'new' control trailer entered service in August 1987 and was often to be found leading at the north end of train formations. Before long, however, it too had its front cab end appearance changed by having its front cab door blocked off for driver comfort. This was not, however, a permanent feature, because if the car was to be used in the middle of a train formation, the cab door would have to be reinstated for emergency access between cars.

Trials were conducted in 1988 into the feasibility of two-car operation in winter months, but in the event it was decided to form one three-car unit which would include a control trailer at one end. CT 28 was chosen for this role and work is seen underway in Ryde workshops in late-1987. The work included re-fitting driving controls and equipment in the cab (all the CTs on the Isle of Wight had their equipment removed a few years previously). *(Brian Hardy)*

Control trailer 28 in its new guise at Shanklin in the summer of 1988. It should be noted that the original 'shutter' headlights have not been reinstated. *(Brian Hardy)*

It wasn't long before the driving cab of CT 28 had to succumb to weather-proofing but, because it may have had to work in the middle of a train formation, the work was not permanent – i.e. the door could be substituted if necessary. The further modified car is seen at Sandown on 2 May 1989. *(Bob Greenaway, LURS Collection)*

Car interiors had, for several years, been repainted in lime green, but when the paint supply ran out, trailer S95 received a mid-grey finish in May 1987. It remained unique in this colour, because five cars that required a stop-gap interior repaint subsequently (in April 1989) were painted in a much brighter 'apple' green. All 11 operational motor cars finished up in Network SouthEast livery, DMs S3, S4 and S11 being repainted directly from the 'grey doors' style to NSE livery – i.e. they were never painted 'Inter City' blue and grey. In contrast, DM S9 which was painted blue and grey in 1986, became NSE-liveried in 1987! A total of 13 trailers were repainted in the new colours but three (S43, S47 and S92) were withdrawn before the repainting programme was completed. The last car so painted was S26 in October 1988, which happened to be the first 'tube' car to arrive on the Isle of Wight on 1 September 1966. Details of all the liveries and internal décor changes are listed in *Appendix 17*.

The interior of a 1923-built Cammell Laird trailer, still retaining its maple wood flooring, but after the replacement of the seating moquette by the type used on LUL's D and 1983 stocks. The luggage pens may be seen on the right and in the background on the left. *(Brian Hardy)*

Interior of 1925 MCCW CT 27, showing that the interior paintwork is now light green. The car has also been rewired and the light fittings relocated to along the centre of the ceiling. The tubing that contains the new wiring also serves as additional grab rails along the cars. *(Brian Hardy)*

Interior of a 1931/34 DM car, still with BR's blue moquette, but after the introduction of the green interior paint scheme. DM cars had one luggage pen as seen on the left, while the 'box' on the left-hand draught screen contains emergency equipment. *(Brian Hardy)*

When the supply of green paint for the interiors ran out, grey was used, but only on 1923 Cammell Laird trailer 95 as seen here complete with lighting modifications. Note that the original flooring has been replaced by linoleum. *(Brian Hardy)*

By now, however, the remaining cars of Pre-1938 Tube Stock were fast approaching the end of their operational lives. No longer was further refurbishment a viable option – an extensive rebuild was the only answer and this was prohibitively expensive. The replacement trains – they arrived during 1989 and 1990 – will be described in the next chapter. During 1989, the fleet was reduced to 17 vehicles, often by reducing five-car sets to four and by disbanding units.

By August 1990, just two operational sets were available for service (2-26-49-7 and 28-31-5), both seeing regular service alongside their replacements during the still relatively busy summer season. Once into September, however, only the three-car set remained operational and then only for winter de-icing purposes. It did make occasional passenger runs, the 'last' being recorded as being on 12 January 1991, with the last de-icing run taking place on Sunday afternoon 17 February 1991, this latter also carrying passengers between Ryde Esplanade and Ryde Pier Head for a catamaran connection from the mainland. Prior to that, when the de-icing runs were made at night, it was not unknown, on occasions, for it to carry passengers along the Pier for the 23.45 ex-Portsmouth catamaran service – which had no booked rail connection!

DM 2 (ex-LT 3706) stands outside the depot at Ryde St John's Road on 16 April 1990. Only a handful of cars of Pre-1938 Tube Stock then remained in service, being replaced by 1938 Tube Stock (some cars of which were only five years younger). The depot at Ryde was adapted for the 'new' stock, which included raising one of the depot roads to provide side access in the shed. *(Bob Greenaway, LURS Collection)*

Only one interior was repainted grey, and when further cars needed repainting, a deeper 'apple green' shade was used instead, as illustrated on this 1931/34 DM looking towards the equipment compartment. *(Brian Hardy)*

A feature of the Pre-1938 Tube Stock (and previous builds of tube stock) DMs was that the equipment was located immediately behind the driver. Access on one side was via opening panels, as seen on DM S13 in the depot yard at Ryde St John's Road in 1982. *(Bob Greenaway)*

For the 1991/92 de-icing season, Unit 28-31-5 was kept in operational condition but the mild winter conditions meant that it was not used. Coupled with the fact that train crews were now 'out of training' on the old stock, it was decided not to maintain it thereafter and thus it lay derelict in the station siding at Ryde St John's Road for another two winters. Although plans were drawn up to convert one unit of the replacement stock for de-icing purposes, the work was undertaken by a diesel-powered Permaquip track maintenance vehicle owned by AMEC Rail and adapted for the role in winter months. In its yellow livery it received the nickname of 'La La', after the children's Teletubby character.

Eventually, cars 28 and 31 were moved to Sandown on 6 April 1994 and cars 5 and 26 the following day. Because car 26 was the very first Pre-1938 tube car to arrive on the island in September 1966, it was intended that it would be preserved by the Isle of Wight Steam Railway. However, the presence of asbestos in the vehicle did not make the cost of the project worthwhile. In Sandown yard, the four cars were broken up, one by one, where several of their predecessors had met their end. DM 5 was the very last to go, on 23 April 1994. The story of the Pre-1938 Tube Stock – on the Isle of Wight at least – is thus concluded.

The withdrawal and scrapping details are listed in *Appendix 18*, in date order of disposal. Readers should, however, be cautious of the withdrawal dates quoted. The actual dates are often at variance with the 'official' records, as will be seen.

The disposal of the remaining Pre-1938 Tube Stock vehicles provides an interesting story. When the withdrawal of the surviving 27 cars began, 23 of them made their way back to the mainland, first being taken to Sandown yard, from where they were taken by lorry on the Fishbourne – Portsmouth ferry to Fratton, being stored in a siding in one long line next to the 'down' side of the station, while decisions were being made about their disposal – a scrap dealer for some and a new home for others.

A total of 18 cars were transferred to Fratton between July 1989 and June 1990, usually as the return workings when replacement 1938 Tube Stock was transferred in. This left five old cars on the island. The scrapping contract for 12 cars (two DMs and ten trailers/CTs) was awarded to Vic Berry of Leicester and all went by road from Fratton during October 1990. Six DM cars, however, went by road back to London Underground at Ruislip depot, to enable equipment parts to be reclaimed for engineers' trains. Here, they languished in a remote siding in the far corner of Ruislip depot near Ruislip siding, to be the victim of graffiti vandals on numerous occasions.

DMs 6 and 9 were subsequently acquired by 'Challenge Films' for a film 'Split Second' and were taken to Abbey Storage in Stepney Way on 1 July 1991. The futuristic film was set in the year 2008 based at 'Cannon Street' station. The two cars had apparently been trapped in the tube for some years following the flooding of London. After filming, the two cars were taken by road on 23 August 1991 to Bird's of Long Marston, for scrap. The four remaining cars remained at Ruislip until collected by Vic Berry of Leicester during January 1993.

The five cars remaining on the island in the summer of 1990 were probably the best in terms of their structural condition and a decision was made to retain them so that a 'heritage' train could be created on the London Underground – 'Museum' trains run in Paris and Berlin (and in some other countries with Metro systems), so why not in London? It has plenty of historical vehicles, but very few that could actually work in service. To that end, the five cars were set aside and two of them were externally repainted into early Underground liveries before they left the Isle of Wight.

Their journey 'home' to London began in the small hours of 1 October 1990 with the movement of the cars from Ryde to Sandown, followed by their transfer on the back of a lorry by ship to Fratton. All had arrived at Fratton by 4 October, but a massive shunting operation was necessary not only to get the five-car train in the formation required for movement by rail to Morden depot open day (2-44-27-49-7), but because the match wagon needed for shunting was next to the buffers on the line of cars waiting to be scrapped. Despite the average age of the train being 60 years, a bold decision was taken for it to run under its own power from Fratton on Network SouthEast (third rail) metals. The transfer day to Wimbledon Park NSE depot was Thursday 18 October 1990 and the route taken was via Haslemere, Guildford, Staines and Clapham Junction, with DM 2 heading the formation for most of the way. The next part of the operation was to get the train to Morden depot in time for the Open Day. Because the train had been working on the BR third rail system for many years, it could not work under its own power on the Underground. The work was thus entrusted to battery locomotives, and then only those that remained fitted with 'Ward' couplers. This was done in two stages, from Wimbledon Park to Ruislip depot on the night of 30 October (where the 'Morden – Edgware Line' transfers were applied), and then from Ruislip to Morden two nights later – arrival at the latter was in the early hours of 2 November, just 31 hours before the public were to be admitted to the depot.

The five-car Vintage Train project saw two trailer cars repainted into early Underground liveries at Ryde workshops before returning to London Underground. 1923 Cammell Laird trailer 44 (ex-7281), at that stage minus numbers and fleetnames, was repainted in 1930s style and awaits departure from Sandown on 3 October 1990. *(Bob Greenaway, LURS Collection)*

The other car to be repainted was former control trailer 27 of 1925 vintage, this being in the 1920s style. It is seen at Fratton having arrived back on the mainland on 3 October 1990, prior returning to London. *(Bob Greenaway, LURS Collection)*

Remarkably, and with great credit to all concerned, the Heritage Train ran under its own power from Fratton. The train is seen being marshalled at Fratton on 3 October 1990, with shunting operations being undertaken by a class 73 electro-diesel. *(Bob Greenaway, LURS Collection)*

The return to London of the five-car train to Wimbledon (and thence to LUL) is seen pausing at Virginia Water. *(Bob Greenaway, LURS Collection)*

The line name as applied to Cammell Laird trailer 7281, along with period notices adjacent to the passenger doors. The Hampstead & City Line became the Morden-Edgware Line in 1933 and Northern Line in 1937. *(Bob Greenaway, LURS Collection)*

1925 MCCW control trailer 5279 displays its original 1920s number in period style on 4 November 1990. *(Bob Greenaway, LURS Collection)*

*Below* The final leg of the journey of the Heritage Train from the Isle of Wight to London Underground for display at Morden was completed in the early hours of 2 November 1990. At 01.15 in the morning, the train is seen reversing in the east-bound Piccadilly Line platform at King's Cross, making its way via the King's Cross loop to the Northern Line at Euston. *(Bob Greenaway, LURS Collection)*

Initially, the cars were made available for public inspection at the Morden depot Open Day on 3 and 4 November 1990, which was arranged to coincide with the Centenary of the Northern Line – the first real 'tube' railway that opened in December 1890 as the City & South London Railway between King William Street and Stockwell. DMs 2 and 7, along with trailer 49 remained in Network SouthEast livery, while 27 was repainted into 1923 colours and 44 in mid-1930s condition.

After the Open Day, the cars remained at Morden depot until 26 March 1991, when they were transferred to Upminster depot for safe-keeping and storage. What was thought to be a final move to Acton Works prior to eventual restoration occurred on 24 November 1991, joining other survivors of this type of stock belonging to London Underground. In 1993, all the remaining Pre-1938 vehicles were allocated to belong to either 'London Underground' or 'London's Transport Museum'. Those five from the Isle of Wight were allocated to the Museum (cars 49 and 27) and London Underground 'Heritage' collection (cars 2, 7 and 44).

When London's Transport Museum 'Depot' project was being set up at the Acton Town end of Ealing Common depot, on the site of the former (but still fairly new) Depot Engineering Support Unit (DESU) building, the two Isle of Wight cars belonging to the Museum were taken to their new home by road on 30 September 1999. There they joined other rail vehicles belonging to the Museum, for which there was no space available at the Covent Garden site.

Whilst a very small amount of work was done on some of the cars at Acton Works (primarily the removal of asbestos), lack of finance has meant that the project has lain dormant for several years. However, an announcement was made by the London Transport Museum in 1998 that it was able to finance the restoration of one car of Pre-1938 Tube Stock, which meant that a future existed for at least some the Isle of Wight cars, with the long-term aim of getting a 'train' back to working condition again. However, the enormity of the project must be appreciated and some of the things that had to be considered were as follows:

- Conversion back to the London Underground four-rail system.
- The train will need two operational driving motor cars (even if a three- or four-car set is made operational) because no train, outside depot limits, is allowed to work on the Underground network with only one air compressor.
- The front cab doors on DMs 2 and 7 have been sealed and will thus need re-instating.
- Whilst the cars have been rewired in recent years, the relocated position of the car lighting along the centre of the ceiling is not the correct position.

These, along with the condition of the bodywork and equipment, the fact that they haven't moved on rails for well over ten years, and the need to incorporate the most stringent of safety features following the King's Cross fire, makes this a truly long-term and costly project – if it is to ever happen.

Whether any further work will be undertaken on any of the Pre-1938 cars to have them ultimately returned to operational condition will be dependent on finance and labour. Some of them do, however, have a secure future in the Museum's collection, even as static displays.

The future for the three LUL-owned cars, however, is far from secure, there being little, if any, enthusiasm or commitment for any true preservation activities, especially in the light of PPP. In 2002–03, moves were being made to dispose of all the Pre-1938 Tube Stock cars at Acton Works (the ex-Isle of Wight cars and the remaining service stock locomotives and Personnel Carriers), but even what might appear to be a simple job of scrapping a small number of carriages was proving to raise problems, including the cost of having them taken away and scrapped!

A line up of Pre-1938 Tube Stock cars at Fratton on 11 April 1990, all of which are awaiting disposal. The majority went to Vic Berry of Leicester. *(Bob Greenaway, LURS Collection)*

Six ex-Isle of Wight tube cars are visible in this view at Vic Berry's scrapyard on 24 November 1990. The cars are 92, 32 and 33 on the ground, 29 on top with 47 and 94 just visible in the background. *(Bob Greenaway, LURS Collection)*

# CHAPTER 3

# IDENTIFICATION OF PRE-1938 STOCK

The Pre-1938 Tube Stock gained the title of 'Standard stock'. This, however, was initially far from the truth, as the many different types built over a period of 12 years made it anything but 'standard' in its early days. Including the six experimental 'sample' cars of 1922, there were 15 distinct batches supplied by six different car builders. Later, many of the cars became operationally compatible.

It is fortunate, certainly from the enthusiasts' point of view, that examples of most types of Pre-1938 Tube Stock were saved for use on the Isle of Wight, in the form of a motor, control trailer or trailer. Cars that were not retained were the 'sample' cars (these had been scrapped in 1954), the 1930 batch that was built specifically for the Bakerloo Line service to Watford, and the six-car experimental train built by the UCC at Feltham around the same time, which was the prototype for the 1931/34 cars.

The 44 cars that went to the island are summarised below in order of age, and are listed in LT-number order.

1. The Isle of Wight received fourteen trailers from a batch built in 1923 by Cammell Laird for the Hampstead & City Line (what is now the Northern Line). Some of these cars were transferred to the Northern City Line in 1939, operating on that line until October 1964, when they were replaced by more modern cars of Pre-1938 Tube Stock. It was fortunate that these cars survived until 1964, for the rest of the type (then on the Central Line) were the first to be scrapped in 1960. The cars had thick waistbands, drop windows, and small rectangular ventilator scoops in sets of three on the curve of the roof line where it meets the clerestory, which had a rounded edge and no eave. The rainstrips immediately above the passenger doors were straight. Unlike the 1922 'Sample' cars, where the clerestory continued along the whole of the roof, the roof was arched over the passenger doors.

| S43S | 7275 | S46S | 7283 | S95S | 7292 |
| S47S | 7279 | S92S | 7285 | S45S | 7293 |
| S42S | 7280 | S41S | 7286 | S49S | 7296 |
| S44S | 7281 | S94S | 7287 | S48S | 7298 |
| S93S | 7282 | S96S | 7290 | | |

The motor bogie of S13S on 17 July 1971 showing the carbon insert in the shoe on the east side of the car. On this side, access to the equipment compartment was via detachable louvres. *(Bob Greenaway, LURS Collection)*

This view of the end of a 1925 MCCW control trailer (left) shows that they lost their all yellow ends in favour of black, as applied to cars repainted in Network SouthEast livery. The ventilator over the front cab door has been patched over, as have the former headcode light shutters. On the right is the end of trailer S93, which was unique on the Isle of Wight in retaining its end grab chains right to the end. *(Bob Greenaway, LURS Collection)*

2. There were nine control trailers from a batch built in 1925 by the Metropolitan Carriage & Wagon Company, also for the Northern Line. This stock marked the end of the first group of Standard stock, all of which had thick waistbands and slightly recessed windows. These were recognisable by having angled ventilator scoops which were largely hidden by the distinctive overhang of the clerestory roof, and ribbed doors with curved rainstrips over them. Five out of the nine cars were used as control trailers in their own right, complete with driving equipment and yellow ends. The other four cars were converted for use as trailers, but the inoperative equipment in the cabs was retained for many years. The cab ends were painted blue.

| S27S | 5279 | S33S | 5291 | S34S | 5302 |
| S31S | 5283 | S29S | 5293 | S28S | 5304 |
| S32S | 5290 | S26S | 5294 | S30S | 5312 |

3. Two driving motors and one control trailer car built in 1927 by the Metropolitan Carriage & Wagon Co. were taken into Isle of Wight service. This type was built for the Piccadilly, Bakerloo and Hampstead & City lines, the three Isle of Wight specimens having worked on several lines over the years. This represented the second generation of the Pre-1938 Tube Stock (although it actually began with the almost identical 1926 stock) and had a smoother appearance than the 1925 (and previous) batches, and was reflected in having no overhang (other than a very small 'lip') to the clerestory roof over the passenger compartments, thus exposing most of the large triangular ventilator scoops. Some of the motor cars had ribbed doors (GEC batch – not used on the Isle of Wight) while others did not (the BTH batch), although on all cars the door panelling was not flush with the frames. The passenger and guard's doors had elliptical rainstrips. On the offside of the switch compartment the ventilator louvres of earlier builds were omitted and plain sheeting used instead. The smoothness of the cars could be noticed by the windows being flush with the bodysides, and the elimination of thick waistbands. The most noticeable difference between the 1927 CT and the 1925 CTs is that the newer car type had all the headlights mounted under the offside cab window with internal shutters, whereas the older cars have four separate headlights, two on each side of the cab and had external shutters.

S25S     3313        S23S     3315        S36S     5350

*Above* All of the control trailers on the Isle of Wight were of 1925 vintage, save for ex-5350 which became S36s. It was built by MCCW in 1927 and is seen at Shanklin in July 1979, photographed from the disused 'up' platform. *(Brian Hardy)*

*Above left* Trailer S29S in original all-blue-livery in the depot yard at Ryde St John's Road. This was one of four former control trailers built in 1925 by MCCW that were put to use on the Isle of Wight as trailers, although the equipment compartment was retained and was not opened up for passenger use as some had been on the London Underground. *(John Herting)*

*Left* 1925 MCCW control trailer S26 in Ryde depot yard, showing that the control trailers 'proper' had yellow driving ends. This is CT S26 in unit 031, which was the first tube car to arrive on the Isle of Wight in September 1966, when it was numbered S38S and was then intended to be in unit 037. *(Brian Hardy)*

4. There were three motor cars on the Isle of Wight that were built in 1928 by UCC Feltham. These were part of a batch built for the Piccadilly and Bakerloo lines and differed from the 1927 MCW cars in that the bodyside bulged slightly, but noticeably below the waist, and the rainstrips over the passenger doors were straight – there was no rainstrip over the guard's door. Most of the UCC motor cars had a centre door pillar (as did the three Isle of Wight examples) and were the last batch of tube cars to be built with these. The decision to do away with centre door pillars was taken during the construction of these cars, hence the fact that the last 20 were delivered without them. No doors had ribbing but the door panels were not flush with the frames.

| | |
|---|---|
| S21S | 3041 |
| S19S | 3045 |
| S20S | 3308 |

5. One 1929 UCC Feltham motor car saw service on the Isle of Wight. This batch of stock was an improvement over the 1928 version, in that the door panels were completely flush with the frames. The ventilator louvres in the roof of the switch compartment were replaced by rectangular covers, which were open at the base and curved with the line of the roof and whose top ends fitted under the clerestory overhang.

| | |
|---|---|
| S22S | 3010 |

6. There were fourteen motor cars, nine built in 1931 for the Piccadilly Line extensions and five built in 1934 for increased Piccadilly Line services, selected for service on the Isle of Wight. The two types were indistinguishable except that in the case of the 1934 cars, the passenger saloon quarter lights were of the lift-to-open type and not spring toggle as on 1931 and previous cars. The 1931/34 cars were the last of the Pre-1938 'Standard' stock to be built. The motor cars had straight panels below the waist, curved rainstrips and a slightly altered front end design. Being slightly longer than their predecessors, the car ends tapered inwards slightly. Above all, these cars were the first, apart from the six-car 1930 UCC prototype, to have air-operated guard's doors, instead of the hand-operated slam type.

| | | | |
|---|---|---|---|
| S8S | 3074 | S15S | 3253 |
| S6S | 3084 | S15S | 3273* |
| S13S | 3141 | S10S | 3696† |
| S5S | 3185 | S4S | 3702† |
| S7S | 3209 | S1S | 3703† |
| S9S | 3223 | S11S | 3705† |
| S3S | 3251 | S2S | 3706† |

* Replacement for original S15S (original number 3073).
† 1934-built car – all others 1931.

Apart from the Heritage Train, all other Pre-1938 Tube Stock cars have been scrapped. These were undertaken at various locations, both on the Isle of Wight and on the mainland. In April and May 1989, seven cars were cut up on site at Sandown. Four of those remaining are seen on 2 May 1989, being DM S20 nearest the camera (the last UCC 'Feltham' car), S15 (the second to bear that number) and trailers S42 and S46. *(Bob Greenaway, LURS Collection)*

Driving motor cars 4 (leading) and 3 are seen on the Oxford By-Pass on 4 October 1990 on their way to Vic Berry's yard in Leicester for scrap. *(Bob Greenaway, LURS Collection)*

# CHAPTER 4

# 1938 TUBE STOCK

Soon after the Pre-1938 Tube Stock on the Isle of Wight had settled down with its new owners, British Rail then had to consider what would replace it, as it was expected to last only a maximum of ten years and the supply of Pre-1938 Tube Stock had been exhausted. The 1938 Tube Stock became available from 1973 but as we have already noted, it was then deemed unsuitable and was rejected.

As it turned out, British Rail decided to continue with refurbishment and improvement programmes on the Pre-1938 Tube Stock, although the fleet reduced through mishaps and service economies. Through frequent fleet examinations, the old trains showed that they could be kept going, but by 1987 it was obvious that the trains would not last much beyond 1990 and the remaining cars were already some ten years beyond their 'sell by' date. Replacement stock thus became more pressing, although the other option – total closure of the railway – was also a strong possibility.

It was fortunate that London Underground did have withdrawn stock available – the 1938 Tube Stock – some 15 years after it was previously rejected. This situation came about because of the increased usage of the London Underground system in the mid-1980s, following a decline and all-time low in passenger numbers in the earlier part of the same decade. This increase in passenger traffic resulted in five seven-car trains of 1938 Tube Stock being refurbished and returned to service on the Northern Line on a short-term basis from September 1986, having previously been withdrawn from the Bakerloo Line in November 1985. The delivery of the 1983 Batch II Tube Stock for the Jubilee Line, the completion of the Bakerloo Line OPO conversion programme and the consequent stock 'cascades' to other lines, saw the 1938 Tube Stock withdrawn (again) in 1988, the last in May. These, however, were the only trains that London Underground had available. The 1959/62 Tube Stock was then projected as not to become available until 1992–93 at the earliest, which was far too long, for what had become Network SouthEast, to wait. In the event, this was overtaken by LUL's decision to replace the Central Line's 1962 Tube Stock, but by then a firm commitment had been made to use 1938 Tube Stock. Nevertheless, with delays in commissioning the 1992 Tube Stock on the Central Line, the first new train did not run until 17 April 1993 and the first bulk withdrawals of 1962 Tube Stock began in the summer of that year, by which time the 1938 Tube Stock had been working for four years on the Isle of Wight.

Fortunately, the closure option for the Ryde–Shanklin line was rejected and Network SouthEast opted for 1938 Tube Stock, whose interesting story is now to be told. Although it was an expensive option, it was far more viable than the prohibitively expensive total rebuild of the older trains.

In April 1988, the 1938 Tube Stock trains were offered to British Rail. The stock available comprised four seven-car trains in more or less complete condition, one four-car unit in partially stripped condition (for scrap) and two Ballast Motors which were no longer required for engineering duties, but were thought to be a useful source of spare parts. London Underground were anxious for the stock to be removed from Ruislip depot, but BR had not decided on the design, layout and the formation of the replacement trains for the Isle of Wight. Indeed, the project had not been authorised and the cars were transferred initially on an 'indefinite loan' basis. Furthermore, with

From Strawberry Hill, the 1938 Tube Stock trains were taken in two-car motor pairs to BRML Eastleigh for conversion for Isle of Wight service between 2-EPB pilots. At the rear of the train and nearest the camera is a 2-EPB unit that began life on the South Tyneside electric lines in the late-1950s. *(Colour-Rail/J.D. Cable)*

the workload at BRML Eastleigh, it was not possible to transfer all the trains directly there. The plan was thus to transfer the cars from Ruislip to the DM&EE depot at Strawberry Hill, where they would be formed into the intended unit formations. There, spare parts would be acquired from the vehicles not required and these would then be dispatched by road to the scrap dealer.

The route taken from Ruislip depot was via Greenford, Ealing Broadway, Old Oak Common, North Pole Junction and Kensington Olympia to Clapham Junction. This part of the transfer was undertaken during the day, but Network SouthEast preferred night time transfers to Strawberry Hill. Thus, the trains remained at Clapham until late in the evening. On the tube cars themselves, some of the brakes were in working order, which avoided the Southern Region ban on unbraked trains. The last train from Ruislip went direct to Strawberry Hill without laying over at Clapham, and the penultimate train went direct to Eastleigh without reforming, to enable BRML to make a start. Details of these initial moves will be found in *Appendix 19*.

Financial authority for the project was granted in October 1988, but preliminary authority had previously been given for investigative work and for an interior mock-up to be undertaken. Given the then non-availability of the 1959 Tube Stock and the politically unacceptable closure option for the Isle of Wight railway, the 1938 Tube Stock was really 'Hobson's choice'.

A later decision resulted in London Underground offering the three-car unit of the 'Starlight Express' train, which was accepted and departed White City for Wimbledon on 11 May 1989 *(Appendix 20)*. The four-car unit of this train, which still has one driving motor car (10012) of the first train in service (on 30 June 1938) was retained and now belongs to London's Transport Museum. It has since been restored to working order and it is hoped may be used on special occasions in the future.

Meanwhile, the trains at Strawberry Hill were formed into two-car (M-M) units and were transferred to Eastleigh in pairs between February and September 1989 *(Appendix 21)*. The formation of each train was as follows:

2-HAP – Match Wagon – 1938 Tube Stock – Match Wagon – 2-HAP

The following year, to enable more spare equipment to be available, seven further redundant 1938 Tube Stock Ballast Motors were offered and were taken by road from Ruislip depot direct to Fratton in October 1990 *(Appendix 22)*.

In April 1988, the conversion work envisaged the minimum that would be compatible with operation on the BR third rail system. Repair work was to be adequate to enable the 1938 Tube Stock to meet service requirements until the 1959/62 Tube Stock became available in around 1995/96 – i.e. a service life of around five years. The feasibility study recommended three-car units but the extension work that would be involved to adapt Ryde Works to take the longer trains would be both technically difficult and extremely costly. Therefore, it was decided to opt for two-car (motor-motor) units, with a maximum of three units per train. The two-car trains were formed up in like-numbered pairs in the same way that they had been on London Transport (e.g. 121-221 were previously 10184-11184). Renumbering and unit formations are as shown in *Appendix 23*.

The change to two-car operation involved the removal of the motor generator set on the 'D' car and replacing it with a compressor. Whilst this might be considered quite a simple exercise, problems arose with the limited space available to fit a compressor, wiring changes and the modifications necessary for third rail operation.

The criteria for the décor and passenger requirements were formulated and two-thirds of one of the 'D' cars first to arrive at Eastleigh was used as a prototype. Summarised, these were:

- Two-car unit operation.
- Maximum operation of six-car trains.
- Conductor/Guard operation.
- Passenger door control (open and close).
- Provision of public address.
- Fitting of fluorescent lighting.
- Heating improvements.
- Exterior Network SouthEast livery.
- Suitable interior décor.

An unidentified 1938 Tube Stock DM car is seen in Eastleigh Works in white undercoat on 9 September 1989. The headlights have been reduced to three and the door push buttons already fitted. *(Bob Greenaway, LURS Collection)*

The Network house style of panelling in two shades of grey was adopted, together with the 'blue blaze' upholstery. However, to avoid a monotony of blue and grey, it was decided to retain the timber mouldings and panels between waist level and the cantrail. The route diagram and advertising space above the cantrail was retained, in the belief that a profitable commercial advertising package could be sold. The panel between the top of this and the roof would incorporate a modified version of lighting used on SR refurbished trains, along with the public address amplifiers.

Apart from the 'busy' summer season, the rail traffic on the Isle of Wight does not justify provision for standing passengers and thus the LUL-style grip handles were removed. However, longitudinal rails were provided over the seated areas, which also provided protection to the fluorescent lighting tubes mounted behind them. No grab rails were fitted in the doorway areas, thus discouraging passengers from standing there. The emergency lighting was located above the doorways, mounted in a flush-mounted fitting.

Early checks of door operation showed that the door rollers were seriously clogged with years of dirt and grease and the door tracks were worn at the centre and clogged with dirt and grease at the inner ends. All door tracks were thus removed with the area cleaned out and corrosion protected. The door tracks were skimmed to remove worn patches and the door rollers cleaned.

To improve the exterior appearance of the roof gutter line, previously filled with mastic and a prime location for corrosion of the roof panels, a metal sheet bridged the space, spot-welded to the outer surface of the gutter and joined tangentially to the roof. Large holes were cut into the old roof to ventilate the enclosed space.

Despite their age, the condition of the body structure was generally extremely good and far better than on some vehicles built in more recent years. Corrosion was found where the roof panels joined the cantrail/gutter line (q.v. above) and particularly over the side cab doors, at bodyside pillars. It was also found on the waist rail at corners of the main windows where the putty had cracked, and in expected locations on the floor sheeting, such as the cab floor and adjacent doorways.

To guard against corrosion in the salt atmosphere, the opportunity was taken to paint all exposed steel surfaces with a bitumen-based paint.

The 1938 stock units for the Isle of Wight became class 483 and unit 483.006 is seen at Eastleigh on 5 June 1990 on a test run. *(Bob Greenaway, LURS Collection)*

It was originally intended that the 1938 Tube Stock would be converted to last for around five years, but during the early phase of the work a number of factors had come to a head, which resulted in the anticipated length of the life of the stock being reconsidered – and subsequently extended. The most significant and important of these was the publication of the Fennell Report into the King's Cross fire. As a result, changes were necessary for the 1938 Tube Stock, summarised as follows:

- The ceiling panels were considered a fire hazard and were replaced by polyester-coated aluminium panels.
- The beech wood mouldings had to be replaced. Fire-resistant treated ash was used instead.
- The LT grooved floor lagging was replaced by linoleum laid on fire resistant multiply bedded on a bitumen coating to inhibit corrosion of the floor sheets. By the door-way areas, this created a 'dip' in the floor level and became a water trap. From the fourth unit onwards, the floor panels were levelled out to eliminate a water 'well' forming during inclement weather.
- The main car windows were found to be loose and leaking to an unacceptable degree for a surface railway running out over the sea. All were to be removed and rebedded in mastic. All non-toughened glass was replaced.
- The tilting quarter lights were fitted with anti-draught strips.
- The floor covering used in the seating areas was grey-flecked linoleum but in the doorway areas a ribbed treadmaster covering was used. The seat risers on the longitudinal seats were covered with a stainless steel kicking strip. Wherever possible, seat frames and painted surfaces were either nylon coated or covered in plastic laminate.

This resulted in the cost of the project increasing considerably, but the expected life of the stock was extended to ten years as a result of these additional and improved features. Consequently, when the 1962 Tube Stock became available from 1993, it was not required for Isle of Wight service and thus most of it went to the scrap yard, despite being some 25 years younger.

London Underground rolling stock is built for fourth rail operation. The traction current return is taken to a negative shoe and is insulated from earth. The Pre-1938 Tube Stock had white metal suspension bearings, so that it was a simple task to connect the negative return to the traction motor carcass. The 1938 Tube Stock, however, has roller bearings throughout, and return of the traction current through these is unacceptable. Fitting of earth brushes to the suspension tubes was considered but discarded because of the work content and risk of laying a copper earth track on the axle, plus the risk of distortion when welding a brush housing on the suspension tube. It was instead decided to fit axle and earth brushes on both ends of two axles on each vehicle, but to make way for these, the existing thrust pad arrangement had to be displaced. There had been a long-standing problem with these thrust panels, so it was decided to fit a new inner bearing sleeve and a ball location race to take the end thrust, retaining the existing bearing outer races where possible. This left the axle ends free to accept the earth brush assemblies and, on one axle, a speedometer drive.

The axleboxes were changed over to grease lubrication. The change to the axlebox arrangement had introduced complications to the shoebeam, and the change in the auxiliary arrangements introduced supply complications during 'gapping' (when a train stops where there is no current rail), and it was thus decided to eliminate the shoegear on the trailing bogie of each vehicle and provide a through power jumper. On each car, the two shoes are connected together on the bogie and are then connected to two power fuses, which were originally the positive and negative equipment fuses. One of these fuses supplies the traction equipment and the other is connected to the inter-coach jumper. The auxiliaries are supplied from the jumper side of the inter-coach jumper on the 'A'-end car. Also fitted to the 'A' car is the SR type shed jumper for traction and an auxiliary shed jumper with changeover switch, the latter supplying the auxiliaries only, without energising the power line, the traction equipment or the shoegear.

For fourth rail operation, the control circuits connected to the traction supply were insulated from earth, the low voltage control and auxiliary circuits were not, and local earth connections for low voltage return circuits were used at many locations on the vehicles.

On a third rail system, all these earth return circuits are in parallel with the traction return and can carry traction return current. Under certain circumstances, particularly if poor track bonding exists, these currents can be large enough to cause malfunctioning of equipment such as brake valves, relays and door valves. It becomes essential to ensure that all control and auxiliary circuits have return connections insulated from the traction supply.

Initially it was intended to use the existing coach wiring and to introduce the negative returns and other changes as an overlay. When the ducts were opened up and the cables exposed, it was found that the insulation had become hard and brittle, and when the cables were distorted the insulation just fell off. The decision to rewire was thus taken, and as a result it was sensible to incorporate the changes into the new wiring. As a consequence, the control and auxiliary circuits were completely redesigned.

Historically, the PCM control equipment had a very good reliability record and few changes were considered necessary. However, resulting from the change to the traction current supply arrangements, the potential relay fuse was removed from the auxiliary equipment and fitted to the end of the PCM case. It was now supplied directly from the live side of the line breakers.

The control of weak field was altered so that the flag switch was removed and in the 'forward 1' position of the controller, not only is a low accelerating current achieved, but both weak field notches are inhibited. In 'forward 2' a higher accelerating current is obtained and the equipment notches right through to the second weak field notch. The change was achieved by adding a weak field relay to the equipment.

To limit damage from the loose gravel ballast and also possibly sea water splashing up, a protective sheet was fitted under the starting resistor grids. Whilst removed from the cars, the equipment was given a thorough overhaul.

The car lighting was supplied from the 'A' car, so that the only equipment in the auxiliary case were the compressor contactor, heading contactor and the brake contactors, along with the 750 volt fuses. The supply for the auxiliaries was via an auxiliary HT jumper from the 'A' car.

On the 'A' car the major changes were the fitting of the battery on the underframe and the mounting at the leading end of the centre bay of a 2kW static inverter to convert the 50V d.c. low voltage supply from the motor generator to 240V 50Hz, to supply the fluorescent lights, the heater fans and the headlights. The MG voltage regulator of the vibrating carbon type had given problems in service and was replaced by a modified version of the solid state regulator developed for the Southern Region's 70V MG sets.

Experience showed that the coach heating provided by a tube car would be inadequate on a surface railway, if any attempt was to be made to meet modern comfort standards. The structure and layout of the 1938 Tube Stock made it extremely difficult to fit in additional convector heaters, and the only space available was under the transverse seats. The arrangement adopted was a blower heater mounted into the back of the transverse seat by the doorways and blowing into the doorway vestibule. The heaters provided were 2kW rating each, a total of 8kW which, with the 3.6kW of convector heating already fitted, provided an improvement that was to be welcomed in the winter months. The fans operate from the a.c. auxiliary supply and the static switch for the element is energised from the same supply. To guard against suitcases being put in front of the heater outlets and causing overheating, the heaters are provided with thermal safety cut-outs. The convector heaters and the element supply to the fan heaters are controlled by a thermostat working on ambient air temperature and is outside train crew control. The operation of the fans is under the guard's control and can thus be used in the summer months to disturb the air. A similar blower heater arrangement is provided in the driver's cab.

Door controls were based on original principles, but passenger operation was incorporated. The control panels were removed from the 'D' cars, so the guard's operating position is always to be found on an 'A' car, even if this is leading on a two-coach formation. The opening of the passenger doors requires the guard's door to be already opened and for two buttons to be pushed, either one by the guard and one by the passenger for passenger operation, or two by the guard for all-door (non-passenger) operation. Push buttons are provided at each doorway position and inside the cars a door-close facility has been provided.

Whilst the conversion work undertaken on the trains was considerable, a lot of work also needed to be done to Ryde Works. For the older trains, it had one level road and one 'pitted' road. The former could accommodate a two-car train but the other track could only accommodate one car comfortably over the inspection pit. With the replacement 1938 Tube Stock, it was necessary to provide a pitted road of two-car length, with side pits, for use as a lifting road. Another major problem to be overcome was with the drainage system, in that the depot was susceptible to flooding from a stream running alongside.

The tracks into the depot were on a falling gradient, so it was possible to bring the track into the old flat road on the level and mount it on supports inside the shed, enabling good side access to the equipment. A shallow pit between the supports provided full access to the underside of the train. Further, the old pitted road was refurbished and the whole depot area resurfaced. Finally, on 17 July 1990, a new carriage cleaning area was commissioned in the depot yard. Train washing hitherto was restricted to a hosepipe and basic 'mop and bucket' facilities in the bay platform at Ryde St John's Road.

The last train to leave Ruislip depot (on 12 November 1988) and be transferred directly to BRML Eastleigh via Clapham was the first to arrive there for conversion. The mock-up work undertaken on one of the 'D' cars has been previously mentioned, and when agreement was reached on the final design, work began on the first two motor-motor pairs, followed by the others as they arrived from Strawberry Hill (six units) or Wimbledon (one unit).

The first two-car unit was ready for its first test run on 30 June 1989, which took place on the main line between Eastleigh and Winchester. Prior to that on 12 June 1989, two motor cars (10229+11229) were formed between a pair of two-car EMUs for a gauging trip between Strawberry Hill and Fratton, as crew training was to later take place between the latter and Haslemere. On 4 July 1989 the first unit was transferred from Eastleigh via Woking to Fratton, in readiness for its shipping to the Isle of Wight, the two cars being loaded onto the lorries the same afternoon. Late that night they moved to the Gunwharf car ferry terminal at Portsmouth, and in the early hours of the following morning the two cars made their way to the island, being unloaded in Sandown yard around midday. The first two-car unit arrived in Ryde Works the following morning, 6 July 1989, having been hauled there by five cars of Pre-1938 Tube Stock. Late that same evening, when the main daytime 'busy' service had been thinned out, the unit made its first test runs.

The official ceremony to inaugurate the 1938 Tube Stock was held on Thursday 13 July 1989 at Ryde Pier Head in the 'shuttle' platform, where unit 483.001 was the star attraction. It had worked specially from the depot and broke a banner placed

The first of the 1938 Tube Stock arrived on the Isle of Wight on 5 July 1989. DM 121 (ex-10184) has arrived at Sandown and is awaiting off-loading before being transferred to its new home at Ryde. *(Bob Greenaway, LURS Collection)*

across the platform on arrival. At the launch, which also marked the beginning of 'Gala Week' on the island, it was interesting to hear that Network SouthEast planned to keep one of the old trains for special trips and winter de-icing, but only if a sponsor could be found to maintain it – sadly this came to nothing. Track improvements were also promised, for while the 1938 Tube Stock rode well on the mainland track, on the Isle of Wight the ride was 'lively', mainly because of the track's shingle base. Once the ceremony at Ryde had been completed, the 'new' train then took invited guests to Brading, to mark the restoration of the station and for the handover of the disused signal frame to the Isle of Wight Steam Railway. On the way, the train paused at the site of the proposed new station at Smallbrook Junction, which would offer interchange with the Isle of Wight Steam Railway. For the rest of the afternoon and on other days of Gala Week, unit 483.001 worked passenger trips on the Ryde Pier shuttle service. Thereafter, for a number of weeks, the unit worked many test trips before being passed for passenger service throughout the line.

The second unit underwent its first test run from Eastleigh on 7 September 1989 and was transferred to Fratton on 15 September. This unit was used for crew training between Fratton and Haslemere, which began three days later. Other units followed on to Fratton after completion at Eastleigh up to May 1990. One car of the third unit was still in white undercoat when it ventured out onto the main line for the first time on 22 September 1989. Work on the fourth and fifth units was such that each was incorrectly paired with each other's motor car partner – i.e. 124+225 and 125+224. The former was ready by the end of November 1989, the latter in January 1990. Both went from Eastleigh to Strawberry Hill (as one four-car train) on 29 January 1990 for brake tests on the Shepperton branch, which began on 5 February after an initial gauging run three days previously. Transfer to Fratton, for onward shipping to the island, was directly from Strawberry Hill on 8 March 1990. They entered service in correct formations in May 1990.

Apart from some test running to and from Eastleigh, the 1938 Tube Stock also worked crew training trips (on the Portsmouth main line) and brake tests (on the Shepperton branch). Unit 483.002 on one of the former is seen in the middle platform at Haslemere on 20 September 1989. *(Fred Ivey)*

The original plan was for eight two-car units of 1938 Tube Stock on the Isle of Wight. This left a pair of motor cars in otherwise good condition at Eastleigh and it was later decided to have a ninth unit, plus two spare coach bodies. To that end, work began on motor cars 10229+11229 to form the ninth unit for passenger service. This pair were the last cars to leave Strawberry Hill for Eastleigh on 12 September 1989. They were not completed until the spring of 1992. The two spare coach bodies were in fact from the unit that had been partially stripped at Ruislip depot and they were nothing much more than 'shells' on bogies. The windows were plated over and they were painted in blue livery, save for yellow 'cab' ends. These made their way to the Isle of Wight in April 1992 with the ninth unit but it was never really expected that they would ever be used for service. They spent most of their time in the long siding south of Ryde St John's Road station. These four cars were not transferred from Eastleigh to Fratton via the usual route via Woking, but the opportunity was taken to use the newly electrified and more direct route via Botley.

A summary of all the movements of the 1938 Tube Stock from completion at Eastleigh on the mainland will be found in *Appendix 24*.

It was not until the autumn of 1989 that the 1938 Tube Stock first began regular passenger service between Ryde and Shanklin *(Appendix 25)*. This followed the extensive testing of the first unit 483.001 and the arrival of the second and third units on the island in late-September. A test of a six-car train of 1938 Tube Stock took place (units 001+002+003) on 2 October 1989, but such formations have never been used in passenger service (apart from very occasional special circumstances), four cars being the maximum.

Some small detail differences existed with some units in the early days of the 1938 Tube Stock on the Isle of Wight. Unit 483.001 had the yellow painted cab front right down to floor level and was extended slightly around the cab corners, while units 002–007 had the yellow painted section end neatly at the corners, and had a thin grey-painted section at floor level. Unit 483.008 was outshopped similarly to 002–007, but the yellow front went right down to floor level. This was altered to have the thin grey line added in June 1990 at Ryde Works, before entering passenger service at the end of the month. The unique-looking unit 001 was painted to standard in February 1993.

The initial 34 cars of 1938 Tube Stock sold to BR for possible use on the Isle of Wight in fact grew to 44, with other additions, comprising the following:

Initial 34 cars –
        9 'A' DMs
        9 'D' DMs
        9 Trailers
        5 NDMs
        2 Ballast Motor cars
Three cars from the 'Starlight Express' –
        1 'A' DM
        1 'D' DM
        1 Trailer
Additional cars –
        7 Ballast Motor cars

Out of the 44 cars of 1938 Tube Stock that left LUL for the Isle of Wight project, only 20 were actually sent to the island, of which 18 were for passenger service and two as spare bodies. Those not required were eventually scrapped. A Ballast Motor car (left) and cars of redundant 1938 Tube Stock can be seen at Strawberry Hill on 31 July 1990. Apart from one NDM scrapped at Eastleigh, all other cars not required were sent to Fratton and taken by road for scrap. *(Bob Greenaway, LURS Collection)*

NDM 12087 and trailers 012227 and 012307 are at Fratton on 9 July 1971 awaiting disposal. *(Bob Greenaway, LURS Collection)*

This line-up of nine 1938 Tube Stock cars at Fratton on 9 July 1971 includes former passenger stock, along with Ballast Motor cars in yellow and maroon liveries. L142 is nearest the camera. *(Bob Greenaway, LURS Collection)*

A total of 20 DM cars went to the Isle of Wight, 18 in two-car motor-motor pairs, plus the two motor car body shells *(Appendix 26)*. There thus remained 24 cars to be disposed of (ten trailers, five NDMs and nine Ballast Motors). One NDM was cut up at Eastleigh by BRML but all the other 23 were sent by road from Fratton to scrap dealer D.G. Corbin in Wimborne, Dorset. This required the transfer of 20 cars from Strawberry Hill to Fratton, and three cars from Eastleigh to Fratton. The seven Ballast Motor cars, which had gone directly from Ruislip to Fratton by road, had previously been sent to Strawberry Hill for the acquisition of spare parts, so they had to make their way back to Fratton before disposal. DMs 10139 and 11172 were used as 'pilots' between the SR units. The standard routeing was taken, via Woking, but for the last transfers, the route was via Botley. Details of these 24 cars can be seen in *Appendix 27*.

The first unit of 1938 stock on the Isle of Wight, 483.001, was different from the others in that the yellow front continued on the corners and right down to the bottom at the front. It is seen leading a four-car train into Ryde St John's Road. *(Brian Hardy)*

A number of modifications have been made to the 1938 Tube Stock trains since being on the Isle of Wight. The first occurred between March and December 1992, when all nine units received red armrests, replacing the original blue. Between November 1994 and March 1995, eight 'A'-end DMs were equipped with guard's equipment boxes, at the expense of two fewer passenger seats. The DM not so treated was 125, which by then had been withdrawn from service (q.v. below). From July 1999 the remaining operational cars were fitted with master controllers from 1959 Tube Stock. The modifications and livery variations are summarised in *Appendix 28*.

It has already been noted that units 004 and 005 were misformed at Eastleigh. This remained the case until transfer to the Isle of Wight, when the correct pairs were formed. Units 003 and 004 also exchanged motors between June 1990 and October 1991, when defects on differing cars resulted in a serviceable unit being formed of cars 124+223. The flooding of Ryde Works in early January 1994 resulted in units 004 and 009 being reformed, making a serviceable unit with 129+224 until 8 February 1994. Two days later, DM 125 was involved in a collision with the stops at Ryde Pier Head, causing some cab damage. Also out of service at the same time was unit 003 with defects and a serviceable unit was formed with 123+225, the unit being officially renumbered 483.003 in December 1994, the out of service unit becoming 483.005. As was soon experienced with the small Pre-1938 Tube Stock fleet over 20 years previously, any losses through mishaps are difficult, if not impossible, to replace. Thus, the new unit 005 (125+223) was the first of the 1938 Tube Stock to be withdrawn, reducing the fleet by one to eight two-car sets.

The passenger usage on the Isle of Wight, although healthy during the summer period, had not warranted the use of the spare coach bodies to replace the damaged cars. Moreover, further defects and a re-appraisal of the railway's needs has resulted in the operational fleet being reduced to just six units. In May 1995 cars 123 and 221 were withdrawn while from June 1996 cars 121+222 were withdrawn, leaving six two-car units for service as follows:

| | | | |
|---|---|---|---|
| 483.002 | 122+225 | 483.007 | 127+227 |
| 483.004 | 124+224 | 483.008 | 128+228 |
| 483.006 | 126+226 | 483.009 | 129+229 |

Details of all unit formation changes to date can be found in *Appendix 29*.

The standard finish to the 1938 Tube Stock in Network SouthEast livery was as illustrated here on unit 483.009 at Sandown on 25 August 1996. The yellow ends just above the bottom and is in line with the black surrounding the cab windows. *(M.W. Johnson)*

A night-time view of a four-car train pausing for business at Sandown heading for Ryde on 12 September 1990. *(M.W. Johnson)*

Unit 483.008 also differed from the rest of the fleet initially, by having the yellow end right down to solebar level, but this was corrected before it entered passenger service. The unit is seen in Ryde workshops in June 1990. *(Brian Hardy)*

Unit 483.008 is seen departing Ryde Pier Head on 20 May 1991 after having its yellow front curtailed short of solebar level. *(Paul Bradley)*

The first unit, 483.001, became 'standard' on its first repaint in February 1993, but had a short life and was withdrawn in June 1996. It was then deemed that six two-car units were sufficient to provide the service (including spares), a far cry from 1967 when 6x7-car trains were required on summer Saturdays. DM 121 stands off-bogies (with other withdrawn cars) in the yard at Ryde St John's Road in the summer of 1998, and was one of four cars scrapped in April 2000. *(Bob Greenaway, LURS Collection)*

Interior of 1938 Tube Stock as modified for Isle of Wight service, looking towards the driving cab. The cars have been fitted with fluorescent lighting and passenger open/close facilities which, unlike those on the London Underground, are still used. Red armrests replaced the blue armrests in 1992. *(Brian Hardy)*

The Isle of Wight fleet would therefore not be increased beyond those six units then being maintained for service. By the end of February 1998, six cars were lifted from the depot into the spare land beside the 'up' line at Ryde St John's Road, pending their disposal. The six cars comprised 121, 125, 222 and 223, along with the two body shells in all-blue livery. Cars 123 and 221 have been retained at Ryde Works for use as stores vehicles, although it could be possible to return either of them to service, should any serious damage occur to a car in the rest of the fleet. The Pier shuttle, which had not operated for some time, was reinstated for the summer season in 1997, but only when a spare train crew was available. Not surprisingly, this was short-lived.

A modification made in 1994-95 was the fitting of emergency equipment boxes by the guard's position, at the expense of two passenger seats. This view also illustrates the red armrests and the guard's control panel. *(Capital Transport)*

The line between Ryde and Shanklin was part of British Rail's Southern Region network, but in 1986 it became Network SouthEast. The replacement 1938 Tube Stock trains had 'Island Line' logos from when they began service on the island from 1989, but it was not until 1 April 1994 that this title was officially adopted in preparation for privatisation. This occurred on 13 October 1996 when a five-year franchise was awarded to Stagecoach, a company probably more well known for its bus operations, although its operation of South West Trains in its early days did not go unnoticed in the media. The Isle of Wight franchise was a unique agreement, in that it would also be responsible for the trackbed. This resulted in a contract being awarded to Amec Rail to maintain track and signalling. Unlike other rail franchises, that for the Isle of Wight was rather short-term. Expiring on 12 October 2001 it was hoped that the franchise would be extended for a further two years, which would see it through the summer season in 2003, and this indeed happened.

In the meantime, it was decided that the next heavy overhaul and repainting programme (in 1998) would involve a change of livery. Various suggestions were made as to what styles should be adopted and with only six operational units, a different one was suggested for each. The new livery in fact took a long time coming, but throughout the time it took to reach a final decision, it was never in doubt that one two-car unit would be repainted back to original 1938 Tube Stock colours, including the cream pillars between the saloon windows. The liveries suggested for the other five units were:

- Southern Region malachite green.
- British Rail all-blue.
- British Rail 'Inter City' blue and grey.
- Stagecoach livery (a modified version of that used on class 442).
- An all-over-advert livery.

In the event, it was decided that five units would receive a themed livery. The base colour was blue (with grey roof and yellow half-front cab ends), to which were added 'dinosaur' decals to recognise the Isle of Wight's reputation for dinosaur fossil discoveries over the years – the more cynical see the 'dinosaur' livery representing the 'age' of the trains. The livery change was funded by the lessors HSBC Rail, and details can be found in *Appendix 30*.

The original Network SouthEast livery was replaced by the current 'Dinosaur' livery on five out of the six operative units in 2000. It is basically an all-blue livery on which dinosaur decals have been added. All five units have been given names, although only 002 displays it. This appears in place of the destination in this view at Sandown! *(Capital Transport)*

The repainting was undertaken after a £1-million electrical and mechanical overhaul of the trains. The first painted unit, 006, was launched in a ceremony at Ryde St John's Road depot on 21 March 2000. In addition to the repainting and addition of dinosaur decals, the destination boxes have been utilised to sport appropriate names. These are: Raptor (002), T-Rex (004), Terry (006), Iggy (008) and Bronti (009).

This left unit 007 still in Network SouthEast livery and this was taken out of traffic for its (LT-style) repaint on 12 May 2000, the last unit to run in NSE colours. It was duly repainted into London Transport colours during August 2000 and then awaited completion of outstanding electrical and mechanical work, before a 'launch' of this 'heritage' unit. Unit 483.007 comprises DMs 10291 and 11291, which were part of the three-car 'Starlight Express' train with London Underground, having featured on the last day of that stock in service on the Bakerloo Line (on 20 November 1985) and similarly on the Northern Line (19 May 1988). Unfortunately, the launch was overtaken by events. The Ryde St John's Road area is susceptible to flooding and the depot had already been 'hit' in early-January 1994 and again at Christmas 1999. Neither event was too serious – the former led to a temporary formation (129–224) for a month, while the latter resulted in a six-car train being operated to Ryde Pier Head on 27 December to move stock away from the depot.

A more serious flood occurred on 9/10 October 2000, not only at Ryde St John's Road, but in the Smallbrook area as well, where track ballast was washed away, causing services to be suspended for a few days. Four out of the six operational units in the depot were flooded to a greater or lesser degree (002, 004, 006 and 007), with only 008 (stabled on the 'raised' track inside the depot) and 009 (stabled at Ryde Pier Head) escaping damage. Unit 004 was returned to service on 13 October, having successfully had its motors dried out, while units 002 and 006 required complete motor replacements (from London Underground at Acton). Unit 006 returned to traffic on 3 December 2000 and 002 on 20 June 2001.

An interior view of a 1938 stock train on the Isle of Wight looking out, showing that the dinosaur decals have also been applied over some of the windows. When the stock was new some 65 years ago, the positions of the line diagrams and advertisements was reversed. A new design of seating moquette is planned. *(Capital Transport)*

Sadly, the unit to suffer the most damage was 007 in LT livery, which had not re-entered service following its repaint and was on the lowest track level in the depot at the time, suffering the brunt of the water damage. Initially, it was thought that the unit may not run again, but repair was eventually decided upon, although the quicker repair option of transferring the two cars back to LUL at Acton by road and ferry was discounted on cost grounds. The flood-damaged components from unit 007, which comprised the entire underside structure at one end, had to be shipped to the REW at Acton for repair, together with the axle boxes at the other end. Despite these best efforts, the return to service of unit 007 was plagued with further ill fortune. Priority had to be given to unit 006 which was in need of a major overhaul which took the returned components intended for 007. A second serious flood delayed the project further with brakes, motors and bogies damaged. In addition, when the unit was stabled outside the depot to make room for more urgent and routine work on the other trains, it was badly covered by graffiti on no fewer than four occasions.

Towards the end of 2002 all the repaired equipment was re-fitted to unit 007, by which time the finishing touches were being completed. To make the train as authentic as possible, correct London Transport bodyside branding and numerals were applied – the cars carry their original numbers. 'A'-end DM 127 is now 10291 once again, while 'D'-DM 227 is 11291. The unit still features the Island Line '007' identification on the cab fronts at either end. Although the train is fitted with high intensity headlights, it was deemed necessary for the cab fronts to bear the mandatory yellow warning panels required by today's operating practices and requirements.

As part of the refurbishment, the unit has been re-varnished and the car windows feature authentic London Transport 'No-Smoking' signs. These, together with the bodyside lettering and numerals, were provided by Tern & Sons and were fixed to the cars by local firm Fuhrmann Signs (who were also responsible for applying the Dinosaur vinyls to the other five trains in the fleet in 2000).

Conductor Guard operation now plays an important part on the Island Line, which avoids the need for most ticket offices to be regularly staffed, with tickets being issued using the portable machine seen in this view. Cycles are carried on the Island Line at no charge, subject to a maximum of four per train and only in the south end. *(Capital Transport)*

A side view of a four-car northbound train at Sandown showing the base blue livery, over which decals have been added to the body sides, over some of the car windows and up onto the curve of the roof. *(Capital Transport)*

A close-up view of the passenger open and close facilities provided on the Island Line trains when converted at Eastleigh. The 1938 stock had passenger open push buttons from new but were taken out of use by 1960, following spasmodic use. *(Capital Transport)*

The sixth unit was chosen to be repainted back into the London Transport colours carried when the stock was new. This was applied to the two 'Starlight Express' DM cars (127-227) in August 2000 but serious flooding of the depot and rolling stock, graffiti attacks and more urgent work on the other units meant that it was 27 January 2003 before the unit re-entered passenger service, following a 'launch' three days previously. *(Brian Hardy)*

And so, in fully restored and resplendent condition 10291+11291 (alias unit 483.007) was 'launched' on 24 January 2003, being the last of the flood-damaged units to re-enter service, some 27 months after the first flood. It entered normal passenger service on 27 January 2003. Details of the flood-damaged units can be found in *Appendix 31*.

A more recent modification made to the remaining fleet of 1938 Tube Stock trains on the Isle of Wight has been the fitting of tripcocks, as an additional safety feature should a train overrun a red signal at the entrance to single line sections. The principle is exactly the same as on the London Underground, in that if a train should pass a signal at danger, the tripcock will strike the signal's trainstop, air will be vented and the train brought to an emergency stop. This was first trialled on unit 483.006 in September 2000, but it was February 2002 before it was introduced on the Island Line, mainly because of the more pressing need to return the 'flooded' units to service. Dates of this modification will be found in *Appendix 32*.

Further experiments were undertaken in connection with winter de-icing arrangements in the latter part of 2002 as an alternative to the Permaquip vehicle hitherto noted. Unit 483.009 was fitted with equipment for spraying de-icing fluid in November 2002 and was successfully tested and demonstrated in the depot yard at Ryde. It was then fitted to 483.004 for the 2002–03 winter season.

The unusually short five-year franchise, as already mentioned, was due to expire on 12 October 2001 and the fact that the trains, then 60–61 years old, would not last much longer, concentrated the official minds wonderfully. It was appreciated that the £1-million rehabilitation and repaint of 1999–2000 would enable the trains to continue until 2003, by which time the railway's infrastructure would need huge investment to continue operation in its current form. This was despite the fact that track and signalling work had been recently undertaken, which resulted in the lifting of some speed restrictions that had been in place for a lengthy period of time.

For many years, the 'busy' service on the Isle of Wight has been a timetable operating at alternate 20/40-minute intervals, but even on Mondays to Fridays, there is an hour interval in the early-afternoon. At least during the summer period, some trains have been blessed by comprising two units. An hourly service continues to suffice in the evenings and on winter Sundays. In the summer season of 2001, however, a 20-minute service was provided on Saturdays, commencing on 21 July. For this, all five operational units were required for service (the sixth, 007, was still out of service with flood damage). A 20-minute summer Saturday service also operated in 2002 and in 2003. As this book closed for press, authorisation had been given to repaint unit 483.009 in LT red, similar to 007, which will enable a four-car train in LT red to operate.

# CHAPTER 5
# THE FUTURE?

Back in 1966, when the Newport and Cowes route was closed, a company called Sadler Vectrail was formed by Charles Sadler Ashby, who planned to revive the line between Ryde and Cowes using light railcars. Despite falling rail traffic at the time, it is believed that the proposal could have worked but with much less staff than what is required for a full-size railway. However, its downfall was twofold – (1) because the local council wanted the trackbed for road improvements in the Newport area (such were the transport priorities then), and (2) British Railways themselves were regarded as resentful of another operator probably making a success of the railway when they could not.

The failure of this scheme led to the Isle of Wight Steam Railway (formed as the Wight Locomotive Society in 1966) acquiring the lease of the Wootton – Haven Street section, themselves having to move out of their temporary base in Newport in January 1971. They established themselves at Haven Street, which is now the 'centre' of the Steam Railway, and began public operation in May 1971. The Isle of Wight Steam Railway extended from Haven Street to Smallbrook Junction on 20 July 1991 with the intermediate station at Ashey opening on 2 May 1993.

Over the years, many proposals have been put forward for the future of rail services on the Isle of Wight. Some schemes could be dismissed as 'inappropriate' or too outlandish, but the huge cost that would be involved in renewing the infrastructure and replacing ageing trains, even on just 8½ route miles of track, make the possibility of light rail, electric or otherwise, more viable in the long term. For this, London Underground rolling stock would be far from suitable, although there were a number of withdrawn trains set aside for specific future LUL projects. The transition of the Underground to Public-Private Partnership (part-Privatisation) meant that at best the trains remained laying idle and gathering dust (and graffiti). By the spring of 2002, with almost all of the 1959/62 Tube Stock scrapped, the stock still available in stored condition were some units of 1972 MkI type from the Northern Line and the fleet of 1983 Batch II stock from the Jubilee Line, neither being suitable for light rail. Most of the latter type were in fact scrapped during 2002 and into 2003.

Other proposals for the Island Line have included linking the electric railway with the Isle of Wight Steam Railway at Smallbrook, to enable steam trains to be operated through to Ryde, and the installation of a south-to-west curve at Smallbrook. In a 'light rail' scheme, the planners envisage a service onwards to Ventnor and via the Steam Railway to Newport and Cowes.

To enable the Island Line to continue operating in its current form, at least until 2003, when both the trains and infrastructure would become life expired, Stagecoach, the operator of the Island Line franchise, negotiated with the Strategic Rail Authority for the franchise to be extended for two years. To that end, the extension was granted, which would expire on 27 September 2003.

But still uppermost in everyone's minds was the future beyond 2003. The Isle of Wight Council, whilst recognising the importance of what little remains of the railway network, is equally realistic about the costs involved. To continue with 'heavy rail' beyond 2003 on a like-for-like replacement would be prohibitively expensive and unrealistic. Moreover, earlier in 2000 the Strategic Rail Authority made a suggestion that the Isle of Wight Council could oversee the franchise in the future, even though the IWC had no experience and little knowledge in operating or managing a railway, as small as it is. The SRA described the Island Line as 'unique' and 'not part of the national Network' and the re-drawn franchise map showed the Isle of Wight without a railway. This was indeed unfortunate!

It may be, therefore, that if heavy rail is not an option, then light rail might be the answer. The parent company, Stagecoach, were involved with the tram system in Sheffield, which has become a hugely successful operation under them. Conversion to a guided busway has also been spoken about. Other proposals, for an extension to Ventnor, reopening to Newport and Cowes and a south to west curve at Smallbrook, are just pipe dreams at the moment.

A feasibility study into the potential life of the 1938 Tube Stock has revealed that it could continue much as the Pre-1938 Tube Stock did – for many years beyond its planned Isle of Wight life.

A report of September 2001 on the future of the Island Line outlined a number of possible options under four headings, which are summarised as follows:

## NO CHANGES TO INFRASTRUCTURE
The exisiting rolling stock could be retained until 2014 and then replaced by withdrawn Underground stock. Alternatively, replacement stock could be obtained in 2004 from LU. Service enhancements could be undertaken to provide a 30-minute service to Shanklin and two pier shuttle trains per hour.

## HEAVY RAIL INVESTMENT RETAINING 3RD RAIL
This included replacing the existing fleet in 2004 and opting for One-Person Operation. Track upgrade would enable a 10-minute Metro-style service on Ryde Pier and a 30-minute Shanklin service. The Brading passing loop would be reinstated and on summer Saturdays additional services could be operated. Another final option would be for a 15-minute service between Ryde Pier Head and Shanklin with two-car trains, but with some four-car formations on summer Saturdays.

## LIGHT RAIL OPTIONS
Provide new light rail vehicles in 2004 operating on the 3rd rail system and extend into Shanklin town centre using overhead line equipment. Another alternative would be to convert the whole system to overhead line operation, which would include the extension into Shanklin town centre.

## DIESEL LIGHT RAIL
These options would see the system de-electrify and new diesel light rail vehicles operate, which would include the extension into Shanklin town centre. This would also incorporate the enhanced service options hitherto described.

Irrespective of all this, any 'vision' for rail transport on the Isle of Wight needs to be turned into commitment, and that can only be done with money. And so far, very little of this has materialised. Not suprisingly, therefore, the option chosen is 'do minimum', which involves retaining the existing trains (now approaching 65 years old), renewing infrastructure only when required and maintaining the existing service levels (at the rather inconvenient 20/40-minute operating pattern).

On 12 November 2002, the Strategic Rail Authority announced that Stagecoach would continue to run the Island Line beyond September 2003 until February 2007. The future of the Island Line is thus assured – for a few more years. With the extended franchise expiring in February 2007, it will be interesting to see whether tube trains on the Isle of Wight will actually survive to mark 40 years of electric traction on the island – on 20 March 2007.

# APPENDICES – PRE-1938 TUBE STOCK

**APPENDIX 1 – 12 cars from London Transport to Southern Region:**

14.08.64  3074 3141 3253 3702 3703 3706 7159 7166 7167 7173 7181 7189  Ruislip-Wimbledon
16.08.64  3074 3141 3253 3702 3703 3706 7159 7166 7167 7173 7181 7189  Wimbledon-Micheldever

**London Transport Withdrawal Dates (all ex-Piccadilly Line):**

| | | | | | | |
|---|---|---|---|---|---|---|
| 26.03.64 | 7189 | | | 20.05.64 | 7173 | |
| 29.04.64 | 7167 | | | 03.06.64 | 3074 | 3141 | 3253 |
| 11.05.64 | 7159 | 7166 | 7181 | 30.07.64 | 3702 | 3703 | 3706 |

**APPENDIX 2 – 61 Cars available ex-Northern City Line after 04.10.64 – at Ruislip:**

| | | | | | | | | | | |
|---|---|---|---|---|---|---|---|---|---|---|
| 3009 | 3010 | 3028 | 3033 | 3035 | 3037 | 3040 | 3041 | 3044 | 3045 | 3047 |
| 3062 | 3064 | 3288 | 3292 | 3301 | 3303 | 3308 | 3311 | 3313 | 3314 | 3315 |
| | | | | | | | | | | |
| 5248 | 5262 | 5270 | 5273 | 5277 | 5279 | 5281 | 5283 | 5285 | 5287 | 5289 |
| 5290 | 5291 | 5293 | 5294 | 5296 | 5302 | 5304 | 5312 | 5350 | 5412 | |
| | | | | | | | | | | |
| 7029 | 7275 | 7276 | 7277 | 7279 | 7280 | 7281 | 7282 | 7283 | | |
| 7285 | 7286 | 7287 | 7290 | 7292 | 7293 | 7295 | 7296 | 7298 | | |

**APPENDIX 3 – 32 cars ex-Northern City Line, October 1964, available at Ruislip January 1965 and moved from Ruislip via Wimbledon to Micheldever between May and July 1965:**

Ruislip to Wimbledon:

| | | | | | | | |
|---|---|---|---|---|---|---|---|
| 14.05.65 | 3033 | 3047 | 3308 | 3311 | 5279 | 5302 | 7283 | 7292 |
| 01.06.65 | 3028 | 3292 | 3301 | 5283 | 5290 | 7282 | 7285 | 7287 |
| 12.07.65 | 3035 | 3044 | 5248 | 5291 | 5296 | 5350 | 7280 | 7286 |
| 23.07.65 | 3037 | 3303 | 3314 | 5293 | 5304 | 5312 | 7275 | 7293 |

Wimbledon to Micheldever:

| | | | | | | | |
|---|---|---|---|---|---|---|---|
| 16.05.65 | 3033 | 3047 | 3308 | 3311 | 5279 | 5302 | 7283 | 7292 |
| 03.06.65 | 3028 | 3292 | 3301 | 5283 | 5290 | 7282 | 7285 | 7287 |
| 14,07.65 | 3035 | 3044 | 5248 | 5291 | 5296 | 5350 | 7280 | 7286 |
| 25.07.65 | 3037 | 3303 | 3314 | 5293 | 5304 | 5312 | 7275 | 7293 |

**APPENDIX 4 – 29 cars ex-Northern City Line, October 1964, at Ruislip August 1965:**

| | | | | | | | | | | |
|---|---|---|---|---|---|---|---|---|---|---|
| DM | 3009 | 3010 | 3040 | 3041 | 3045 | 3062 | 3064 | 3288 | 3313 | 3315 |
| CT | 5262 | 5270 | 5273 | 5277 | 5281 | 5285 | 5287 | 5289 | 5294 | 5412 |
| T | 7029 | 7276 | 7277 | 7279 | 7281 | 7290 | 7295 | 7296 | 7298 | |

**APPENDIX 5 – Cars selected and rejected – March 1966:**

**(a) 10 cars stored at Micheldever and rejected –**

| | | | | | | |
|---|---|---|---|---|---|---|
| DM | 3028 | 3033 | 3044 | | Noted at Wimbledon on 19.03.67 |
| CT | 5248 | | | |
| T | 7159 | 7166 | 7167 | 7173 | 7181 | 7189 |

**(b) 12 replacement cars selected at Ruislip –**

| | | | | | |
|---|---|---|---|---|---|
| DM | 3010 | 3041 | 3045 | 3313 | 3315 |
| CT | 5294 | | | | |
| T | 7279 | 7281 | 7290 | 7295 | 7296 | 7298 |

**(c) 17 cars rejected at Ruislip –**

| | | | | | | | | |
|---|---|---|---|---|---|---|---|---|
| DM | 3009 | 3040 | 3062 | 3064 | 3288 | | | |
| CT | 5262 | 5270 | 5273 | 5277 | 5281 | 5285 | 5287 | 5289 | 5412 |
| T | 7029 | 7276 | 7277 | | | | | |

## APPENDIX 6 – 25 selected cars returned to LT ex-Micheldever:

| DM | 3074 | 3141 | 3253 | 3308 | 3702 | 3703 | 3706 | | |
|----|------|------|------|------|------|------|------|---|---|
| CT | 5279 | 5283 | 5290 | 5291 | 5293 | 5302 | 5304 | 5312 | 5350 |
| T  | 7275 | 7280 | 7282 | 7283 | 7285 | 7286 | 7287 | 7292 | 7293 |

**Note:**

| 3141 | 3308 | 3702 | 5350 | 7280 | 7286 | Ex-Micheldever 17.05.66 |
|------|------|------|------|------|------|--------------------------|
| 3074 | 3253 | 3703 | 3706 | 5279 | 5291 | Ex-Micheldever 24.05.66 |

Other dates not known

---

## APPENDIX 7 – Cars rejected in September 1966:

**(a) 1 car stored at Micheldever and rejected, September 1966 -**

| CT | 5296 |
|----|------|

**(b) 8 cars stored at Micheldever rejected September 1966 and later returned to Ruislip -**

| DM | 3035 | 3047 | | | | |
|----|------|------|---|---|---|---|
| DM | 3037 | 3292 | 3301 | 3303 | 3311 | 3314 |

**(c) 1 car rejected September 1966 at Ruislip –**

| T | 7295 |
|---|------|

---

## APPENDIX 8 – Seven replacement DM cars selected from Northern City Line:

Ex-Northern City Line:

| 31.08.66 | 3084 | 3705 |
|----------|------|------|
| 25.10.66 | 3251 | 3696 |
| 26.10.66 | 3185 | |
| 01.11.66 | 3223 | |
| 02.11.66 | 3209 | |

---

## APPENDIX 9 – Transfers from London Transport to Southern Region after overhaul at Acton Works and 3rd rail conversion:

| Dates from Acton Works | Car & B.O. Date | | Car & B.O. Date | | Car & B.O. Date | | Car & B.O. Date | |
|------------------------|------|----------|------|----------|------|----------|------|----------|
| 13.05.66 | 3010 | 12.05.66 | 3313 | 12.05.66 | 7283 | 12.05.66 | 7296 | 12.05.66 |
| 10.06.66 | 3045 | 10.06.66 | 5294 | 10.06.66 | 7279 | 10.06.66 | | |
| 08.07.66 | 3315 | 07.07.66 | 3702 | 07.07.66 | 7281 | 07.07.66 | 7290 | 07.07.66 |
| 18.08.66 | 3041 | 17.08.66 | 5291 | 17.08.66 | 5350 | 17.08.66 | | |
| 08.09.66 | 3141 | 07.09.66 | 3308 | 07.09.66 | 5279 | 07.09.66 | 7286 | 07.09.66 |
| 29.09.66 | 3074 | 27.09.66 | 3703 | 27.09.66 | 5293 | 07.09.66 | 7280 | 07.09.66 |
| 20.10.66 | 3253 | 06.10.66 | 3706 | 06.10.66 | 5283 | 06.10.66 | 7275 | 06.10.66 |
| 07.11.66 | 3084 | 23.11.66 | 3705 | 23.11.66 | 7293 | 23.11.66 | 7298 | 23.11.66 |
| 01.12.66 | 5304 | 17.12.66 | 7282 | 17.12.66 | 7285 | 17.12.66 | | |
| 05.01.67 | 3251 | 17.12.66 | 5290 | 17.12.66 | 5312 | 17.12.66 | 7287 | 17.12.66 |
| 26.01.67 | 3185 | 17.12.66 | 3696 | 17.12.66 | 5302 | 17.12.66 | | |
| 16.02.67 | 3209 | 19.02.67 | 3223 | 19.02.67 | 7292 | 19.02.67 | | |

BO: Body Overhaul

## APPENDIX 10 – Renumbering by Southern Region:

### DRIVING MOTOR CARS:

| IoW No. | Ex-LT No. | Type | Into Set |
|---|---|---|---|
| S1S | 3703 | 1934 MCW | 031 |
| S2S | 3706 | 1934 MCW | 043 |
| S3S | 3251 | 1931 MCW | 032 |
| S4S | 3702 | 1934 MCW | 044 |
| S5S | 3185 | 1931 MCW | 033 |
| S6S | 3084 | 1931 MCW | 045 |
| S7S | 3209 | 1931 MCW | 034 |
| S8S | 3074 | 1931 MCW | 046 |
| S9S | 3223 | 1931 MCW | 035 |
| S10S | 3696 | 1934 MCW | Spare |
| S11S | 3705 | 1934 MCW | 036 |
| S12S | Renumbered S22S before entering service | | |
| S13S | 3141 | 1931 MCW | 041 |
| S15S | 3253 | 1931 MCW | 042 |
| S15S | 3273 | 1931 MCW | 042 |
| S17S | Renumbered S21S before entering service | | |
| S19S* | 3045 | 1928 UCC | 043* |
| S20S | 3308 | 1928 UCC | 041 |
| S21S | 3041 | 1928 UCC | 044 |
| S22S | 3010 | 1929 UCC | 042 |
| S23S | 3315 | 1927 MCW | 045 |
| S25S | 3313 | 1927 MCW | 046 |

| | |
|---|---|
| MCW | Metropolitan Carriage & Wagon Co. |
| UCC | Union Construction & Finance Co. (Feltham) |
| CL | Cammell Laird & Company |

### CONTROL TRAILERS:

| IoW No. | Ex-LT No. | Type | Into Set |
|---|---|---|---|
| S26S | 5294 | 1925 MCW | 031 |
| S28S | 5304 | 1925 MCW | 032 |
| S30S | 5312 | 1925 MCW | 033 |
| S32S | 5290 | 1925 MCW | 034 |
| S34S | 5302 | 1925 MCW | 035 |
| S36S | 5350 | 1927 MCW | 036 |
| S38S* | Renumbered S26S before entering service | | |

### TRAILERS (EX-CONTROL TRAILERS):

| IoW No. | Ex-LT No. | Type | Into Set |
|---|---|---|---|
| S27S | 5279 | 1925 MCW | 041 |
| S29S | 5293 | 1925 MCW | 042 |
| S31S | 5283 | 1925 MCW | 043 |
| S33S | 5291 | 1925 MCW | 044 |

### TRAILERS:

| IoW No. | Ex-LT No. | Type | Into Set |
|---|---|---|---|
| S41S | 7286 | 1923 CL | 041 |
| S42S | 7280 | 1923 CL | 042 |
| S43S | 7275 | 1923 CL | 043 |
| S44S | 7281 | 1923 CL | 044 |
| S45S | 7293 | 1923 CL | 045 |
| S46S | 7283 | 1923 CL | 046 |
| S47S | 7279 | 1923 CL | 031 |
| S48S | 7298 | 1923 CL | 045 |
| S49S | 7296 | 1923 CL | 046 |
| S92S | 7285 | 1923 CL | 032 |
| S93S | 7282 | 1923 CL | 033 |
| S94S | 7287 | 1923 CL | 034 |
| S95S | 7292 | 1923 CL | 035 |
| S96S | 7290 | 1923 CL | 036 |

Note * First formed as set 037, disbanded before entering service.

## APPENDIX 11 – ISLE OF WIGHT TRAIN FORMATIONS

### Proposed formations of IoW stock for 46 cars - not used:

| Set | 'A'-end DM | T | T | 'D'-end DM |
|---|---|---|---|---|
| 041 | S10S | S27S | S41S | S1S |
| 042 | S2S | S29S | S42S | S21S |
| 043 | S12S | S31S | S43S | S3S |
| 044 | S4S | S33S | S44S | S23S |
| 045* | S14S | S48S | S45S | S5S |
| 046 | S6S | S49S | S46S | S25S |
| Spare: | S8S | | | |

| Set | 'A'-end DM | T | 'D'-end DM |
|---|---|---|---|
| 031 | S26S | S91S | S7S |
| 032 | S28S | S92S | S9S |
| 033 | S30S | S93S | S11S |
| 034 | S32S | S94S | S13S |
| 035 | S34S | S95S | S15S |
| 036 | S36S | S96S | S17S |
| 037* | S38S | S47S | S19S |

Note *

These units did exist briefly before the stock entered service on the IoW

# Initial stock formations on the Isle of Wight for 43 cars:

| | 'A'-end | | | 'D'-end |
|---|---|---|---|---|
| Set | DM | T | T | DM |
| **Four-car Units - 4-VEC:** | | | | |
| **041** | S20S | S27S | S41S | S13S |
| **042** | S22S | S29S | S42S | S15S |
| **043** | S2S | S31S | S43S | S19S |
| **044** | S4S | S33S | S44S | S21S |
| **045** | S6S | S48S | S45S | S23S |
| **046** | S8S | S49S | S46S | S25S |
| **Spare:** | S10S | | | |

| | 'A'-end | | 'D'-end |
|---|---|---|---|
| Set | DM | T | DM |
| **Three-car Units - 3-TIS:** | | | |
| **031** | S26S | S47S | S1S |
| **032** | S28S | S92S | S3S |
| **033** | S30S | S93S | S5S |
| **034** | S32S | S94S | S7S |
| **035** | S34S | S95S | S9S |
| **036** | S36S | S96S | S11S |

Each four-car unit as initially formed comprised one 1927-29 DM and one (slightly longer) 1931/34 DM to ensure that all trains were of uniform length.

---

## APPENDIX 12 – Dates of entry into service on Isle of Wight:

| | |
|---|---|
| 20.03.67 | Units 031, 032, 042, 044 & spare car S10S |
| 22.03.67 | Units 036 & 046 |
| 26.04.67 | Units 034 & 035 |
| 15.05.67 | Unit 045 |
| 20.05.67 | Units 033 & 043 |

---

## APPENDIX 13 – Additional cars from London Transport (Ruislip) to SR (Micheldever)

| | | | | | | | |
|---|---|---|---|---|---|---|---|
| 09.07.68 | 3082 | 3310 | 3312 | 5270 | 5273 | 5277 | 5285 |

---

## APPENDIX 14 – Disposal of rejected cars:

### (a) Scrapped at Ruislip by Birds of Long Marston –

| 05.06.67 | 3040 | 3288 | 5289 | 7277 | | | |
|---|---|---|---|---|---|---|---|
| 23.11.67 | 3028 | 3037 | 3303 | | | | Returned to Ruislip ex-Micheldever |

### (b) From Ruislip to Birds of Long Marston by rail –

| 19.06.67 | 3009 | 3062 | 3064 | | | | |
|---|---|---|---|---|---|---|---|
| 19.06.67 | 3314 | | | | | | Returned to Ruislip ex-Micheldever |
| 03.07.67 | 3033 | 3035 | 3047 | 3292 | 3301 | 3311 | Returned to Ruislip ex-Micheldever |
| 22.08.67 | 7276 | | | | | | |
| 27.09.67 | 5262 | 5281 | 5287 | 7029 | | | |
| 27.09.67 | 3044 | | | | | | Returned to Ruislip ex-Micheldever |
| 11.12.67 | 5412 | 7295 | | | | | |

### (c) From Micheldever to Birds of Long Marston by rail –

| 14.09.68 | 5248 | 5296 | 7159 | 7166 | 7167 | 7173 | 7181 | 7189 |
|---|---|---|---|---|---|---|---|---|
| 11.08.70 | 3082 | 3310 | 3312 | 5270 | 5273 | 5277 | 5285 | |

**APPENDIX 15 – Subsequent (known) changes to train formations:**

| Unit | From | | | | Unit | To | | | | Total Cars For Service |
|------|------|------|------|------|------|------|------|------|------|------|
| **Original Formations** | | | | | | | | | | |
| **031** | 26 | 47 | 1 | | | | | | | |
| **032** | 28 | 92 | 3 | | | | | | | |
| **033** | 30 | 93 | 5 | | | | | | | |
| **034** | 32 | 94 | 7 | | | | | | | |
| **035** | 34 | 95 | 9 | | | | | | | |
| **036** | 36 | 96 | 11 | | | | | | | |
| **041** | 20 | 27 | 41 | 13 | | | | | | |
| **042** | 22 | 29 | 42 | 15 | | | | | | |
| **043** | 2 | 31 | 43 | 19 | | | | | | |
| **044** | 4 | 33 | 44 | 21 | | | | | | |
| **045** | 6 | 48 | 45 | 23 | | | | | | |
| **046** | 8 | 49 | 46 | 25 | | | | | | |
| **Spare** | 10 | | | | | | | | | |
| | | | | | | | | | | **43** |

**1968**

| Unit | From | | | | Unit | To | | | |
|------|------|------|------|------|------|------|------|------|------|
| **032** | 28 | 92 | 3 | | **042** | 10 | 28 | 92 | 3 |
| **042** | 22 | 29 | 42 | 15 | **032** | 22 | 29 | 42 | |

15 ex-042 damaged beyond repair, unit 042 temporary reno 032.
10 ex-spare to 032 and unit 032 temporary reno 042 **42**

**1971 (1)**

| Unit | From | | | | Unit | To | | | |
|------|------|------|------|------|------|------|------|------|------|
| **046** | 8 | 49 | 46 | 25 | **046** | 8 | 49 | 46 | 15 |

Replacement '15' used in 046 in place of 25 until September 1971. **43**

**1971 (2)**

| Unit | From | | | | Unit | To | | | |
|------|------|------|------|------|------|------|------|------|------|
| **042** | 10 | 28 | 92 | 3 | **032** | 28 | 92 | 3 | |
| **032** | 22 | 29 | 42 | | **042** | 22 | 29 | 42 | 15 |
| **046** | 8 | 49 | 46 | 15 | **046** | 8 | 49 | 46 | 25 |

Units 032/042 reverted to normal with replacement '15' ex-046.
Replacement '15' ex-046 to 042, 10 ex-temporary 032 to spare. **43**

**1974**

| Unit | From | | | | Unit | To | | | |
|------|------|------|------|------|------|------|------|------|------|
| **035** | 34 | 95 | 9 | | **045** | 6 | 34 | 95 | 9 |
| **045** | 6 | 48 | 45 | 23 | | | | | |
| **036** | 36 | 96 | 11 | | **035** | 36 | 96 | 11 | |

48, 45 & 23 ex-045 withdrawn, 34, 95 & 9 ex-035 to 045.
Unit 036 becomes 035 and unit 036 disbanded. **40**

**1976**

| Unit | From | | | | Unit | To | | | |
|------|------|------|------|------|------|------|------|------|------|
| **034** | 32 | 94 | 7 | | **034** | 10 | 32 | 94 | 7 |
| **034** | 10 | 32 | 94 | 7 | **034** | 32 | 94 | 7 | |
| | | | | | | | | | **40** |

**1980**

| Unit | From | | | | Unit | To | | | |
|------|------|------|------|------|------|------|------|------|------|
| **046** | 8 | 49 | 46 | 25 | **036** | 8 | 49 | 46 | |

25 ex-046 withdrawn, remains of unit 046 becomes 036 and unit 046 disbanded. **39**

## 1982

| 033 | 30 | 93 | 5 | | 043 | 2 | 31 | 43 | 5 |
| 043 | 2 | 31 | 43 | 19 | | | | | |
| **Spare** | 10 | | | | **Spare** | 10 | 93 | | |

30 ex-033 withdrawn, 19 ex-043 withdrawn, 93 ex-033 to spare, 5 ex-033 to 043.
Unit 033 disbanded.                                                                                 **37**

## 1983

| 031 | 26 | 47 | 1 | | 031 | 26 | 47 | 13 |
| 041 | 20 | 27 | 41 | 13 | 041 | 20 | 27 | 41 | 1 |
| 035 | 36 | 96 | 11 | | 035 | 36 | 96 | 9 |
| 045 | 6 | 34 | 95 | 9 | 045 | 6 | 34 | 95 | 11 |

1 ex-031 to 041, 13 ex-041 to 031. 11 ex-035 to 045, 9 ex-045 to 035.                                **37**

## 1985

| 031 | 26 | 47 | 13 | | 031 | 20 | 11 | | |
| 032 | 28 | 92 | 3 | | 032 | 22 | 15 | | |
| 034 | 32 | 94 | 7 | | | | | | |
| 035 | 36 | 96 | 9 | | | | | | |
| 036 | 8 | 49 | 46 | | | | | | |
| 041 | 20 | 27 | 41 | 1 | 041 | 2 | 26 | 92 | 27 | 1 |
| 042 | 22 | 29 | 42 | 15 | 042 | 4 | 28 | 42 | 29 | 3 |
| 043 | 2 | 31 | 43 | 5 | 043 | 6 | 32 | 43 | 31 | 5 |
| 044 | 4 | 33 | 44 | 21 | 044 | 8 | 49 | 44 | 33 | 7 |
| 045 | 6 | 34 | 95 | 11 | 045 | 10 | 34 | 94 | 93 | 9 |
| **Spare** | 10 | 93 | | | **Spare** | 41 | 46 | 47 | 95 | |

26 ex-031 to 041, 47 ex-031 to spare, 13 ex-031 withdrawn.
3 & 28 ex-032 to 042, 92 ex-032 to 041.
32 ex-034 to 043, 94 ex-034 to 045, 7 ex-034 to 044, unit 034 disbanded.
9 ex-035 to 045, 36 & 96 ex-035 withdrawn, unit 035 disbanded.
8 & 49 ex-036 to 044, 46 ex-036 to spare, unit 036 disbanded.
20 ex-041 to 031, 41 ex-041 to spare, 2 ex-043 to 041.
15 & 22 ex-042 to 032, 4 ex-044 to 042.
6 ex-045 to 043.
95 ex-045 to spare, 10 & 93 ex-spare to 045.
3321 ex-044 withdrawn.
11 ex-045 to 031.                                                                                   **33**

## 1987

| 031 | 20 | 11 | | | 031 | 28 | 11 | | |
| 032 | 22 | 15 | | | 032 | 20 | 15 | | |
| 042 | 4 | 28 | 42 | 29 | 3 | 042 | 4 | 47 | 95 | 29 | 3 |
| **Spare** | 41 | 46 | 47 | 95 | | | | | |

28 ex-042 to 031, 22 ex-032 withdrawn, 20 ex-031 to 032.
42 ex-042 withdrawn, 47 & 95 ex-spare to 042.
41 & 46 ex-spare withdrawn.                                                                          **29**

## 1988

| 032 | 20 | 15 |

Unit 032 disbanded, 15 & 20 withdrawn.                                                               **27**

## 1989 (1)

| 042 | 4 | 47 | 95 | 29 | 3 | 042 | 4 | 95 | 29 | 3 |
| 043 | 6 | 32 | 43 | 31 | 5 | 043 | 6 | 32 | 31 | 5 |

ex-043 & 47 ex-042 withdrawn.                                                                        **25**

**1989 (2)**

| 031 | 28 | 11 | | | | 041 | 2 | 26 | 34 | 1 | |
|-----|----|----|----|----|----|-----|----|----|----|----|----|
| 041 | 2 | 26 | 92 | 27 | 1 | 042 | 4 | 28 | 31 | 29 | 11 |
| 042 | 4 | 95 | 29 | 3 | | 043 | 6 | 95 | 32 | 27 | 5 |
| 043 | 6 | 32 | 31 | 5 | | 045 | 10 | 93 | 94 | 9 | |
| 045 | 10 | 34 | 94 | 93 | 3 | | | | | | |

28 & 11 ex-031 to 042, unit 031 disbanded. 27 ex-041 to 043, 92 ex-041 withdrawn, 34 ex-045 to 041. 95 ex-042 to 043, 3 ex-042 withdrawn, 28 & 11 ex-031 to 042, 31 ex-043 to 042.　　　**23**

**1989 (3)**

| 042 | 4 | 28 | 31 | 29 | 11 | 031 | 28 | 31 | 11 | |
|-----|----|----|----|----|----|-----|----|----|----|----|
| 043 | 6 | 95 | 32 | 27 | 5 | 043 | 6 | 95 | 27 | 5 |
| 044 | 8 | 49 | 44 | 33 | 7 | 044 | 8 | 44 | 49 | 7 |

28, 31 & 11 ex-042 to 031 (unit 031 reinstated), 4 & 29 ex-042 withdrawn and unit 042 disbanded. 32 ex-043 & 33 ex-044 withdrawn.　　　**19**

**1989 (4)**

| 031 | 28 | 31 | 11 | | | | | |
|-----|----|----|----|----|-----|----|----|----|
| 045 | 10 | 93 | 94 | 9 | 045 | 10 | 93 | 94 | 9 |

28 ex-031 to spare, 9 & 94 ex-045 withdrawn, 11 & 31 ex-031 to 045, unit 031 disbanded.　　　**17**

**1989 (5)**

| 041 | 2 | 26 | 34 | 1 | 041 | 28 | 34 | 1 |
|-----|----|----|----|----|-----|----|----|----|

2 & 26 ex-041 to spare, 28 ex-spare to 041.　　　**17**

**1990 (1)**

| 041 | 28 | 34 | 1 | | 041 | 2 | 26 | 34 | 1 |
|-----|----|----|----|----|-----|----|----|----|----|
| 043 | 6 | 95 | 27 | 5 | 043 | 6 | 95 | 31 | 5 |

2 & 26 ex-spare to 041, 28 ex-041 to spare (for re-fitting of centre cab door), 31 ex-045 to 043, 27 ex-043 withdrawn (for LUL), 10, 93 & 11 ex-045 withdrawn – 045 disbanded.　　　**13**

**1990 (2)**

| 043 | 6 | 95 | 31 | 5 | 043 | 10 | 95 | 31 | 5 |
|-----|----|----|----|----|-----|----|----|----|----|
| 044 | 8 | 44 | 49 | 7 | 044 | 8 | 28 | 49 | 7 |

28 ex-spare to 044, 44 ex-044 withdrawn (for LUL), 10 ex-045 reinstated in 043, 6 ex-043 withdrawn.　　　**12**

**1990 (3)**

| 043 | 10 | 95 | 31 | 5 | 043 | 10 | 31 | 5 |
|-----|----|----|----|----|-----|----|----|----|

95 withdrawn　　　**11**

**1990 (4)**

| 041 | 2 | 26 | 34 | 1 | 041 | 2 | 34 | 1 | |
|-----|----|----|----|----|-----|----|----|----|----|
| 043 | 10 | 31 | 5 | | 043 | 10 | 26 | 31 | 5 |

　　　**11**

**1990 (5)**

| 041 | 2 | 34 | 1 | | 043 | 10 | 26 | 31 | 5 |
|-----|----|----|----|----|-----|----|----|----|----|
| 043 | 2 | 26 | 31 | 5 | 044 | 8 | 28 | 49 | 7 |
| 044 | 28 | 49 | 7 | | | | | | |

2 ex-041 to 043, 10 ex-043 withdrawn, 34 & 1 ex-041 withdrawn, Unit 041 disbanded, 8 ex-044 withdrawn.　　　**7**

**1990 (6)**

| 043 | 2 | 26 | 31 | 5 | 043 | 28 | 31 | 5 |
|-----|----|----|----|----|-----|----|----|----|
| 044 | 28 | 49 | 7 | | | | | |

28 ex-044 to 043, 2 ex-043 for LUL, 26 ex-043 withdrawn, 49 & 7 ex-044 for LUL.　　　**3**

## APPENDIX 16 – Changes to Stock Totals

| Year | Units | Spare | Total | +/- Variance |
|------|-------|-------|-------|--------------|
| 1967 | 6x3 6x4 | 1 DM | 43 | |
| 1968 | 6x3 6x4 | | 42 | -15 |
| 1971 | 6x3 6x4 | 1 DM | 43 | +15 (replacement - 3273) |
| 1974 | 5x3 6x4 | 1 DM | 40 | -23, -45, -48 |
| 1980 | 6x3 5x4 | 1 DM | 39 | -25 |
| 1982 | 5x3 5x4 | 1 DM + 1 T | 37 | -19, -30 |
| 1985 | 2x2 5x5 | 4 T | 33 | -13, -21, -36, -96 |
| 1987 | 2x2 5x5 | | 29 | -22, -41, -42, -46 |
| 1988 | 1x2 5x5 | | 27 | -15, -20 |
| 1989 (1) | 1x2 3x5 2x4 | | 25 | -43, -47 |
| 1989 (2) | 2x4 3x5 | | 23 | -3, -92 |
| 1989 (3) | 4x4 1x3 | | 19 | -4, -29, 2, -33 |
| 1989 (4) | 4x4 | 1 CT | 17 | -9, -94 |
| 1989 (5) | 3x4 1x3 | 1 DM + 1 T | 17 | |
| 1990 (1) | 3x4 | 1 CT | 13 | -10, -11, -27, -93 |
| 1990 (2) | 3x4 | | 12 | +10, -6, -44 |
| 1990 (3) | 2x4 1x3 | | 11 | -95 |
| 1990 (4) | 1x4 1x3 | | 7 | -1, -8, -10, -34 |
| 1990 (5) | 1x3 | | 3 | -2, -7, -26, -49 |
| 1991 | Nil | | – | -5, -28, -31 |

## APPENDIX 17 – Livery Changes and Modifications

| Car | Type | IoW 'NEW' Blue livery & interiors Mushroom | EXTERIORS Repaint Grey Doors | Repaint Blue & Grey | Mod Cab End | Repaint N-SE | INTERIOR D Stock Seats | Lime Green Interior | Lino Floor | Vents & Lights Mod | Apple Green Interior |
|-----|------|------|------|------|------|------|------|------|------|------|------|
| S1S | 'D' DM | | 26.01.80 | 04.03.82 | 04.12.85 | 25.04.88 | 22.12.82 | 19.11.81 | 25.04.88 | 04.12.85 | 04.89 |
| S2S | 'A' DM | | 09.12.78 | 06.02.82 | 12.02.86 | 28.02.89 | 28.10.82 | 19.02.82 | 09.03.88 | 12.02.86 | |
| S3S | 'D' DM | | 17.02.79 | | 01.09.87 | 01.09.87 | 21.02.83 | 14.10.81 | 12.05.88 | 01.09.87 | |
| S4S | 'A' DM | | 09.04.77 | | 13.11.87 | 13.11.87 | 02.04.83 | 13.11.87 | 18.04.88 | 13.11.87 | |
| S5S | 'D' DM | | 11.02.78 | 01.02.82 | 06.06.85 | 17.03.88 | 11.11.82 | 22.01.82 | 26.02.88 | 06.06.85 | |
| S6S | 'A' DM | | 27.11.76 | 06.04.86 | 06.04.86 | 15.05.89 | 11.03.83 | 06.04.86 | 01.03.88 | 06.04.86 | |
| S7S | 'D' DM | | 01.05.76 | 02.04.84 | 10.02.88 | 10.02.88 | 27.01.83 | 02.04.84 | 09.02.88 | 10.02.88 | |
| S8S | 'A' DM | | 14.07.79 | 30.01.82 | 29.06.88 | 29.06.88 | 25.11.82 | 07.03.81 | 03.12.82 | 29.06.88 | |
| S9S | 'D' DM | | 11.01.77 | 1986 | 07.02.87 | 07.02.87 | 17.05.83 | 07.02.87 | 03.02.88 | 07.02.87 | 04.89 |
| S10S | 'A' DM | | 15.05.76 | 23.06.86 | 23.06.86 | 20.02.87 | 17.05.83 | 23.06.86 | 26.01.88 | 23.06.86 | |
| S11S | 'D' DM | | 16.10.76 | | 16.06.87 | 16.06.87 | 18.01.83 | 16.06.87 | 05.02.83 | 16.06.87 | |
| S13S | 'D' DM | | 18.09.76 | | | | 11.11.82 | 09.05.81 | | | |
| S15S | 'D' DM | | 10.03.79 | 05.01.83 | 15.01.88 | | 08.12.82 | 05.01.83 | | | |
| S19S | 'D' DM | | 12.04.78 | | | | | | | | |
| S20S | 'A' DM | | 22.03.80 | 17.03.82 | 15.01.88 | | 24.11.82 | 22.05.81 | | | |
| S21S | 'D' DM | | 17.05.77 | 10.03.83 | | | 04.04.83 | | | | |
| S22S | 'A' DM | | 21.01.79 | 03.05.83 | | | 08.12.82 | 28.05.83 | | | |
| S26S | 'A' CT | ALL | 15.01.80 | 12.03.82 | | 11.10.88 | 28.10.82 | 26.09.81 | 22.02.86 | 27.06.85 | |
| S27S | Trailer | CARS | 15.02.80 | 24.03.82 | | 01.06.88 | 23.11.82 | 28.03.81 | 01.06.88 | 12.04.85 | |
| S28S | 'A' CT | | 28.04.79 | 16.07.83 | 15.02.88 | 10.03.87 | 21.02.83 | 12.09.81 | 16.07.83 | 10.03.87 | |
| S29S | Trailer | | 07.10.80 | 23.04.83 | | 22.03.88 | 08.12.82 | 26.07.82 | 18.03.88 | 12.09.86 | |
| S30S | 'A' CT | | 17.12.79 | | | | | | | | |
| S31S | Trailer | | 20.05.78 | 07.04.82 | | 12.05.88 | 28.10.82 | 30.04.82 | 12.05.88 | 17.12.84 | 04.89 |
| S32S | 'A' CT | | 11.05.76 | 19.06.85 | | 03.02.88 | 27.01.83 | 19.06.85 | 01.10.85 | 19.06.85 | 04.89 |
| S33S | Trailer | | 30.07.77 | 10.12.84 | | 12.08.88 | 02.04.83 | 10.12.84 | 18.12.84 | 06.02.87 | |
| S34S | 'A' CT | | 18.06.76 | 21.08.86 | | 29.04.87 | 10.03.83 | 21.08.86 | 29.04.88 | 21.08.86 | |
| S36S | 'A' CT | | 14.08.76 | | | | 18.01.83 | | | | |
| S41S | Trailer | | 11.08.79 | 30.01.82 | | | 25.11.82 | 14.02.81 | | | |
| S42S | Trailer | | 07.04.79 | 26.03.83 | | | 25.11.82 | 13.11.82 | 27.08.82 | | |
| S43S | Trailer | | 26.03.78 | 04.01.82 | | | 28.10.82 | 14.12.81 | 10.04.82 | 20.09.85 | |
| S44S | Trailer | | 03.06.77 | 21.07.84 | | 14.07.88 | 04.04.83 | 21.07.84 | 21.07.84 | 15.10.85 | |
| S46S | Trailer | | 11.08.79 | 30.01.82 | | | 11.03.83 | 14.02.81 | | | |
| S47S | Trailer | | 13.05.80 | 08.03.82 | | | 22.12.82 | 18.06.81 | 13.06.81 | 24.12.86 | |
| S49S | Trailer | | 22.09.79 | 13.02.82 | | 13.09.88 | 11.03.83 | 31.01.81 | 17.10.81 | 07.02.85 | |
| S92S | Trailer | | 12.08.78 | 09.08.83 | | | 21.02.83 | 05.08.81 | 18.07.81 | 12.06.85 | |
| S93S | Trailer | | 28.01.76 | 05.09.83 | | 28.02.87 | 26.04.83 | 07.11.83 | 26.01.84 | 13.11.86 | |
| S94S | Trailer | | 17.04.76 | 19.07.84 | | 03.08.88 | 27.01.83 | 19.07.84 | 03.06.82 | 02.05.86 | 04.89 |
| S95S | Trailer | | 09.07.76 | | | 16.05.87 | 10.03.83 | Note* | 29.01.80 | 16.05.87 | |
| S96S | Trailer | | 18.09.76 | | | | 18.01.83 | | 23.08.80 | | |

*Grey interior 16.05.87. Cars not listed had no detail changes before withdrawal.

## APPENDIX 18 – PRE-1938 TUBE STOCK DISPOSAL

| Car | Type | LT No. | Date Withdrawn | Date to Mainland | Fratton to LUL | Disposal | Cars O/S |
|---|---|---|---|---|---|---|---|
| S15S | 'D' DM | 3253 | 07.10.67 | – | – | 10.05.69 | Scrapped following depot collision on 07.10.67 | 43 |
| S23S | 'D' DM | 3315 | 10.09.73 | – | – | 04.05.74 | Scrapped following collision in Ryde depot on 10.09.73 | |
| S45S | Trailer | 7293 | 10.09.73 | – | – | 04.05.74 | Scrapped following collision in Ryde depot on 10.09.73 | |
| S48S | Trailer | 7298 | 10.09.73 | – | – | 04.05.74 | Scrapped following collision in Ryde depot on 10.09.73 | 40 |
| S25S | 'D' DM | 3313 | 08.09.75 | – | – | Oct-82 | Cut up Ryde depot by BR following fire damage at Ryde depot on 08.09.75 | 39 |
| S13S | 'D' DM | 3141 | Mar-85 | – | – | Jun-87 | Cut up Ryde by Ryde Demolition Co. | |
| S21S | 'D' DM | 3041 | Mar-85 | – | – | Jun-87 | Cut up Ryde by Ryde Demolition Co. | |
| S36S | 'A' CT | 5350 | Mar-85 | – | – | Jun-87 | Cut up Ryde by Ryde Demolition Co. | |
| S96S | Trailer | 7290 | Mar-85 | – | – | Jun-87 | Cut up Ryde by Ryde Demolition Co. | |
| S30S | 'A' CT | 5312 | Dec-82 | – | – | Jul-87 | Cut up Ryde by Ryde Demolition Co. | 34 |
| S19S | 'D' DM | 3045 | Dec-82 | – | – | 21.04.89 | Cut up Sandown by Oxley Thomas | |
| S15S | 'D' DM | 3273 | 11.04.88 | – | – | 08.05.89 | Cut up Sandown by Oxley Thomas | |
| S20S | 'A' DM | 3308 | 11.04.88 | – | – | 08.05.89 | Cut up Sandown by Oxley Thomas | |
| S41S | Trailer | 7286 | 12.09.86 | – | – | 08.05.89 | Cut up Sandown by Oxley Thomas | |
| S22S | 'A' DM | 3010 | 14.11.86 | – | – | 16.05.89 | Cut up Sandown by Oxley Thomas | |
| S42S | Trailer | 7280 | 27.11.86 | – | – | 16.05.89 | Cut up Sandown by Oxley Thomas | |
| S46S | Trailer | 7283 | 14.02.86 | – | – | 16.05.89 | Cut up Sandown by Oxley Thomas | 27 |
| S3S | 'D' DM | 3251 | 1989 | 28.09.89 | – | 04.10.90 | Fratton to V. Berry by road | |
| S4S | 'A' DM | 3702 | 25.09.89 | 28.09.89 | – | 04.10.90 | Fratton to V. Berry by road | |
| S33S | Trailer | 5291 | 20.09.89 | 26.09.89 | – | 13.10.90 | Fratton to V. Berry by road | |
| S92S | Trailer | 7285 | 04.10.88 | 26.09.89 | – | 14.10.90 | Fratton to V. Berry by road | |
| S32S | 'A' CT | 5290 | 04.09.89 | 28.09.89 | – | 15.10.90 | Fratton to V. Berry by road | |
| S29S | Trailer | 5293 | 25.09.89 | 28.09.89 | – | 16.10.90 | Fratton to V. Berry by road | |
| S94S | Trailer | 7287 | 03.10.89 | 13.03.90 | – | 17.10.90 | Fratton to V. Berry by road | |
| S34S | 'A' CT | 5302 | 06.06.90 | 22.06.90 | – | 20.10.90 | Fratton to V. Berry by road | |
| S93S | Trailer | 7282 | 18.01.90 | 16.03.90 | – | 20.10.90 | Fratton to V. Berry by road | |
| S9SS | Trailer | 7292 | 05.03.90 | 14.03.90 | – | 23.10.90 | Fratton to V. Berry by road | |
| S43S | Trailer | 7275 | 30.09.88 | 05.07.89 | – | 25.10.90 | Fratton to V. Berry by road | |
| S47S | Trailer | 7279 | Nov-87 | 05.07.89 | – | 30.10.90 | Fratton to V. Berry by road | 15 |
| S6S | 'A' DM | 3084 | 01.02.90 | 14.03.90 | 10.10.90 | 01.07.91 | Ruislip to old Abbey Storage (Old Watney's Brewery), Stepney Way, E1, thence to Birds Long Marston 23.08.91 by road | |
| S9S | 'D' DM | 3223 | 03.10.89 | 13.03.90 | 09.10.90 | 01.07.91 | | |
| S2S | 'A' DM | 3706 | 07.09.90 | 02.10.90 | 18.10.90 | – | To LUL for Vintage Train project | |
| S49S | Trailer | 7296 | 07.10.90 | 02.10.90 | 18.10.90 | – | To LUL for Vintage Train project | |
| S27S | Trailer | 5279 | 18.01.90 | 03.10.90 | 18.10.90 | – | To LUL for Vintage Train project | |
| S44S | Trailer | 7281 | 03.02.90 | 03.10.90 | 18.10.90 | – | To LUL for Vintage Train project | |
| S7S | 'D' DM | 3209 | 07.09.90 | 04.10.90 | 18.10.90 | – | To LUL for Vintage Train project | |
| S10S | 'A' DM | 3696 | 06.06.90 | 20.06.90 | 11.10.90 | 05.01.93 | Ruislip to V. Berry by road | |
| S1S | 'D' DM | 3703 | 06.06.90 | 20.06.90 | 11.10.90 | 07.01.93 | Ruislip to V. Berry by road | |
| S8S | 'A' DM | 3074 | 06.06.90 | 22.06.90 | 12.10.90 | 08.01.93 | Ruislip to V. Berry by road | |
| S11S | 'D' DM | 3705 | 18.01.90 | 16.03.90 | 09.10.90 | 15.01.93 | Ruislip to V. Berry by road | 4 |
| S28S | 'A' CT | 5304 | 13.05.91 | 31.05.91 | – | 14.04.94 | Cut up Sandown by Gwent Demolition of Margam | |
| S31S | Trailer | 5283 | 13.05.91 | 31.05.91 | – | 16.04.94 | Cut up Sandown by Gwent Demolition of Margam | |
| S26S | 'A' CT | 5294 | 07.09.90 | 04.12.90 | – | 18.04.94 | Cut up Sandown by Gwent Demolition of Margam | |
| S5S | 'D' DM | 3185 | 13.05.91 | 31.05.91 | – | 23.04.94 | Cut up Sandown by Gwent Demolition of Margam | |

N.B. Readers should treat the 'withdrawal' dates with caution, for the official date was often at variance with what really happened, as will be understood when studying the tables!

# APPENDICES – 1938 TUBE STOCK

### APPENDIX 19 - 34 cars ex-Ruislip:

#### (a) Ruislip to Clapham

| | | | | | | | | |
|---|---|---|---|---|---|---|---|---|
| 14.10.88 | 10255 | 012364 | 11255 | 10116 | 012211 | 12087 | 11116 | |
| 21.10.88 | 10229 | 012307 | 11229 | 10142 | 012227 | 12112 | 11142 | |
| 28.10.88 | 10139 | 012259 | 12061 | 11172 | L148 | | | |
| 11.11.88 | 10221 | 012160 | 11221 | 10184 | 012272 | 12123 | 11184 | |

#### (b) Ruislip to Strawberry Hill (direct)

| | | | | | | | | |
|---|---|---|---|---|---|---|---|---|
| 18.11.88 | 10205 | 012292 | 11205 | 10297 | 012378 | 12027 | 11297 | L149 |

#### (c) Clapham to Strawberry Hill

| | | | | | | | |
|---|---|---|---|---|---|---|---|
| 15.10.88 | 10255 | 012364 | 11255 | 10116 | 012211 | 12087 | 11116 |
| 22.10.88 | 10229 | 012307 | 11229 | 10142 | 012227 | 12112 | 11142 |
| 29.10.88 | 10139 | 012259 | 12061 | 11172 | L148 | | |

#### (d) Clapham to BRML Eastleigh

| | | | | | | | |
|---|---|---|---|---|---|---|---|
| 12.11.88 | 10221 | 012160 | 11221 | 10184 | 012272 | 12123 | 11184 |

### APPENDIX 20 – 3 cars ex-White City:

| (a) White City to Wimbledon | | | | (b) Wimbledon to Eastleigh | | | |
|---|---|---|---|---|---|---|---|
| 11.05.89 | 10291 | 012371 | 11291 | 19.05.89 | 10291 | 012371 | 11291 |

### APPENDIX 21 – 12 cars Strawberry Hill to Eastleigh:

| | | |
|---|---|---|
| 03.02.89 | 10116 | 11116 |
| 07.04.89 | 10205 | 11205 |
| 14.04.89 | 10142 | 11142 |
| 28.04.89 | 10297 | 11297 |
| 26.05.89 | 10255 | 11255 |
| 12.09.89 | 10229 | 11229 |

### APPENDIX 22 – 7 Ballast Motors ex-Ruislip to Fratton by road for spares:

| | | |
|---|---|---|
| 09.10.90 | L142 | L143 |
| 10.10.90 | L153 | |
| 11.10.90 | L141 | L152 |
| 12.10.90 | L145 | |
| 15.10.90 | L144 | |

### APPENDIX 23 – Renumbering by BR (N-SE):

| LUL No. | N-SE No. | Unit No. | Date | LUL No. | N-SE No. | Unit No. | Date |
|---|---|---|---|---|---|---|---|
| 10184 | 121 | 483.001 | Jul-89 | 11184 | 221 | 483.001 | Jul-89 |
| 10221 | 122 | 483.002 | Sep-89 | 11221 | 222 | 483.002 | Sep-89 |
| 10116 | 123 | 483.003 | Sep-89 | 11116 | 223 | 483.003 | Sep-89 |
| 10205 | 124 | 483.004 | Nov-89 | 11205 | 224 | 483.004 | Jan-90 |
| 10142 | 125 | 483.005 | Jan-90 | 11142 | 225 | 483.005 | Nov-89 |
| 10297 | 126 | 483.006 | May-90 | 11297 | 226 | 483.006 | May-90 |
| 10291 | 127 | 483.007 | Feb-90 | 11291 | 227 | 483.007 | Feb-90 |
| 10255 | 128 | 483.008 | Apr-90 | 11255 | 228 | 483.008 | Apr-90 |
| 10229 | 129 | 483.009 | Mar-92 | 11229 | 229 | 483.009 | Mar-92 |
| 10139 | 130* | 483.010 | – | 11172 | 230* | 483.010 | – |

**APPENDIX 24 – Mainland Movements:**

| Unit | 'A'-DM | 'D'-DM | | |
|------|--------|--------|---|---|
| 483.001 | 121 10184 | 221 11184 | First test run Eastleigh & Winchester | 30.06.89 |
| | | | Transferred Eastleigh to Fratton via Woking | 04.07.89 |
| 483.002 | 122 10221 | 222 11221 | First test run Eastleigh & Winchester | 07.09.89 |
| | | | Transferred Eastleigh to Fratton via Woking | 15.09.89 |
| | | | First crew training run Fratton & Haslemere | 18.09.89 |
| 483.003 | 123 10116 | 223 11116 | First test run Eastleigh & Winchester | 22.09.89 |
| | | | Transferred Eastleigh to Fratton via Woking | 25.09.89 |

Note that DM 123 ran in undercoat white on first test run.

| Unit | 'A'-DM | 'D'-DM | | |
|------|--------|--------|---|---|
| 483.004/5 | 124 10205 | 225 11142 | First test run Eastleigh & Winchester | end-11/89 |
| | | | Eastleigh to Strawberry Hill for brake tests | 29.01.90 |
| | | | Gauging trip Strawberry Hill & Shepperton | 02.02.90 |
| | | | First of brake test runs (with 125+224) | 07.02.90 |
| | | | Strawberry Hill to Fratton | 08.03.90 |
| 483.005/4 | 125 10142 | 224 11205 | First test run Eastleigh & Winchester | 11.01.90 |
| | | | Eastleigh to Strawberry Hill for brake tests | 29.01.90 |
| | | | Gauging trip Strawberry Hill & Shepperton | 02.02.90 |
| | | | First of brake test runs | 05.02.90 |
| | | | Strawberry Hill to Fratton | 08.03.90 |
| 483.007 | 127 10291 | 227 11291 | First test run Eastleigh & Winchester | 19.02.90 |
| | | | Transferred Eastleigh to Fratton via Woking | 07.03.89 |
| 483.008 | 128 10255 | 228 11255 | First test run Eastleigh & Winchester | 06.04.90 |
| | | | Transferred Eastleigh to Fratton via Woking | 14.06.90 |
| 483.006 | 126 10297 | 226 11297 | First test run Eastleigh & Winchester | 17.05.90 |
| | | | Transferred Eastleigh to Fratton via Woking | 14.06.90 |
| 483.009 | 129 10229 | 229 11229 | First test run Eastleigh & Winchester | 13.03.92 |
| | | | Transferred Eastleigh to Fratton via Botley | 02.04.92 |
| 483.010* | 10139* | 11172* | Transferred Eastleigh to Fratton via Botley | 01.04.92 |

Note * 10139+11172 nominally unit 483.010, cars 130+230 respectively.

---

**APPENDIX 25 – Entered Isle of Wight Service:**

| | | |
|---|---|---|
| 13.07.89 | 121+221 | 483.001 |
| 07.10.89 | 122+222 | 483.002 |
| 07.10.89 | 123+223 | 483.003 |
| 01.05.90 | 124+224 | 483.004 |
| 11.05.90 | 125+225 | 483.005 |
| 18.05.80 | 127+227 | 483.007 |
| 29.06.90 | 128+228 | 483.008 |
| 13.07.90 | 126+226 | 483.006 |
| 18.06.92 | 129+229 | 483.009 |

**APPENDIX 26 – Movements to Isle of Wight:**

| 'A'-DM | 'D'-DM | Detail | Date |
|---|---|---|---|
| 121 10184 | 221 11184 | From Fratton to Portsmouth by road | 04.07.89 |
| | | Shipped Portsmouth to Fishbourne | 05.07.89 |
| | | Unloaded at Sandown | 05.07.89 |
| | | Sandown to Ryde | 06.07.89 |
| | | First test run ex-Ryde | 06.07.89 |
| | | Entered service | 13.07.89 |
| | | Type testing from | 02.08.89 |
| 122 10221 | 222 11221 | From Fratton to Portsmouth by road | 25.09.89 |
| | | Shipped Portsmouth to Fishbourne | 25.09.89 |
| | | Unloaded at Sandown | 26.09.89 |
| | | Sandown to Ryde | 26.09.89 |
| | | First test run ex-Ryde | 28.09.89 |
| | | Entered service | 07.10.89 |
| 123 10116 | 223 11116 | From Fratton to Portsmouth by road | 27.09.89 |
| | | Shipped Portsmouth to Fishbourne | 27.09.89 |
| | | Unloaded at Sandown | 27.09.89 |
| | | Sandown to Ryde | 27.09.89 |
| | | First test run ex-Ryde | 29.09.89 |
| | | Entered service | 07.10.89 |

Note: First four-car IoW test run (001+002) on 1 October 1989.
First six-car IoW test run (001+002+003) on 2 October 1989.

| 'A'-DM | 'D'-DM | Detail | Date |
|---|---|---|---|
| 127 10291 | 227 11291 | From Fratton to Portsmouth by road | 12.03.90 |
| | | Shipped Portsmouth to Fishbourne | 12.03.90 |
| | | Unloaded at Sandown | 12.03.90 |
| | | Sandown to Ryde | 15.03.90 |
| | | First test run ex-Ryde | 14.05.90 |
| | | Entered service | 18.05.90 |
| 124 10205 | 224 11205 | From Fratton to Portsmouth by road | 13.03.90 |
| | | Shipped Portsmouth to Fishbourne | 13.03.90 |
| | | Unloaded at Sandown | 14.03.90 |
| | | Sandown to Ryde | 15.03.90 |
| | | First test run ex-Ryde | 04.04.90 |
| | | Entered service | 01.05.90 |
| 125 10142 | 225 11142 | From Fratton to Portsmouth by road | 15.03.90 |
| | | Shipped Portsmouth to Fishbourne | 15.03.90 |
| | | Unloaded at Sandown | 15.03.90 |
| | | Sandown to Ryde | 16.03.90 |
| | | Entered service | 11.05.90 |
| 126 10297 | 226 11297 | From Fratton to Portsmouth by road | 19.06.90 |
| | | Shipped Portsmouth to Fishbourne | 19.06.90 |
| | | Unloaded at Sandown | 20.06.90 |
| | | Sandown to Ryde | 21.06.90 |
| | | Entered service | 13.07.90 |
| 128 10255 | 228 11255 | From Fratton to Portsmouth by road | 20.06.90 |
| | | Shipped Portsmouth to Fishbourne | 21.06.90 |
| | | Unloaded at Sandown | 22.06.90 |
| | | Sandown to Ryde | 23.06.90 |
| | | Entered service | 29.06.90 |
| (130) 10139 | (230) 11172 | From Fratton to Portsmouth by road | 08.04.92 |
| | | Shipped Portsmouth to Fishbourne | 08.04.92 |
| | | Unloaded at Sandown | 08.04.92 |
| | | Sandown to Ryde | 11.04.92 |
| 129 10229 | 229 11229 | From Fratton to Portsmouth by road | 09.04.92 |
| | | Shipped Portsmouth to Fishbourne | 09.04.92 |
| | | Unloaded at Sandown | 09.04.92 |
| | | Sandown to Ryde | 11.04.92 |
| | | Entered service | 18.06.92 |

## APPENDIX 27 – Movement and Disposal of 1938 Tube Stock cars not required for IoW service

**Disposals shown in bold.**     Other movements shown thus.

\* DMs 10139 & 11172 used as 'pilots' on each move shown thus.

§ DMs 10139 & 11172 transferred also but on end of formation and not specifically as pilots.

| 06.04.90 | **12123** | | | | | | **Cut up BRML Eastleigh** |
|---|---|---|---|---|---|---|---|
| 09.11.90 | L142 | L143 | | | | | Fratton to Strawberry Hill |
| 19.03.91 | L142 | L143 | | | | | Strawberry Hill to Fratton |
| 27.03.91 | L152 | L153 | | | | | Fratton to Strawberry Hill |
| 28.03.91 | *012211 | 012259 | | | | | Strawberry Hill to Fratton |
| 02.05.91 | L141 | L144 | L145 | | | | Fratton to Strawberry Hill |
| 02.05.91 | L152 | L153 | | | | | Strawberry Hill to Fratton |
| 10.05.91 | *012292 | 12087 | | | | | Strawberry Hill to Fratton |
| 23.05.91 | *012227 | 012307 | | | | | Strawberry Hill to Fratton |
| 12.06.91 | *012378 | 12061 | | | | | Strawberry Hill to Fratton |
| 14.06.91 | *012364 | L149 | | | | | Strawberry Hill to Fratton |
| 04.07.91 | L145 | | | | | | Strawberry Hill to Fratton |
| **09.07.91** | **L145** | **L149** | **12061** | **012307** | **012364** | **012378** | **Fratton to D.G. Corbin, Wimborne, Dorset** |
| **10.07.91** | **L152** | **L153** | **12087** | **012227** | **012259** | **012292** | **Fratton to D.G. Corbin, Wimborne, Dorset** |
| 21.08.91 | L141 | L144 | | | | | Strawberry Hill to Fratton |
| 25.09.91 | *12027 | 12112 | | | | | Strawberry Hill to Fratton |
| **23.10.91** | **L141** | **L144** | **12027** | **12112** | **012211** | | **Fratton to D.G. Corbin, Wimborne, Dorset** |
| **24.10.91** | **L142** | **L143** | | | | | **Fratton to D.G. Corbin, Wimborne, Dorset** |
| 11.11.91 | §L148 | | | | | | Strawberry Hill to Fratton via Botley |
| 15.11.91 | *012160 | 012272 | | | | | Eastleigh to Fratton via Botley |
| 17.01.92 | *012371 | | | | | | Eastleigh to Fratton via Botley |
| **05.02.92** | **L148** | **012160** | | | | | **Fratton to D.G. Corbin, Wimborne, Dorset** |
| **06.02.92** | **012272** | **012371** | | | | | **Fratton to D.G. Corbin, Wimborne, Dorset** |

**Summary of Disposals:**

| Ballast Motors | 9 |
|---|---|
| Non-Driving Motors | 5 |
| Trailers | 10 |

---

## APPENDIX 28 – Livery and Detail Changes:

| Date | Unit | Details |
|---|---|---|
| Jun-89 | 483.001 | Ex-BRML Eastleigh with yellow front extended slightly around cab corners and down to bottom of body. |
| 26.06.90 | 483.008 | Ex-BRML Eastleigh with yellow front down to bottom of body. Altered to be as 002-007 in that thin grey line added to bottom of body before entering service. |
| Mar-92 | 483.009 | Ex-BRML Eastleigh and to IoW with no Island Line logo, rain strips over side cab doors are more (but not entirely) straight, and with 'No-Smoking' labels at every saloon window position, including sliding doors. |
| Mar-92 | 483.003 | Red armrests replaced blue |
| Apr-92 | 483.007 | Red armrests replaced blue |
| Nov-92 | 483.001/2/5/8 | Red armrests replaced blue |
| Dec-92 | 483.004/6/9 | Red armrests replaced blue |
| 19.02.93 | 483.001 | Repainted standard as 002-009 |
| 24.11.94 | 483.004 | 'A'-end car 124 with guard's equipment box – less two passenger seats |
| 30.11.94 | 483.002 | 'A'-end car 122 with guard's equipment box – less two passenger seats |
| 17.12.94 | 483.003 | 'A'-end car 123 with guard's equipment box – less two passenger seats |
| 03.02.95 | 483.001 | 'A'-end car 121 with guard's equipment box – less two passenger seats |
| 06.02.95 | 483.006 | 'A'-end car 126 with guard's equipment box – less two passenger seats |
| 09.03.95 | 483.008 | 'A'-end car 128 with guard's equipment box – less two passenger seats |
| 16.03.95 | 483.007 | 'A'-end car 127 with guard's equipment box – less two passenger seats |
| 24.03.95 | 483.009 | 'A'-end car 129 with guard's equipment box – less two passenger seats |
| Jul-99 | 483.009 | Fitted with 1959 Tube Stock master controllers – other units subsequently fitted |

**APPENDIX 29 – Changes to Unit Formations:**

| Date | Unit | From | To | Notes |
|------|------|------|------|-------|
| Nov-89 | 483.004 | | 124+225 | From 'new' |
| Jan-90 | 483.005 | | 125+224 | From 'new' |
| 15.03.90 | 483.004 | 124+225 | 124+224 | Reverts to correct formation |
| 15.03.90 | 483.005 | 125+224 | 125+225 | Reverts to correct formation |
| 29.06.90 | 483.003 | 123+223 | 123+224 | Defective |
| 29.06.90 | 483.004 | 124+224 | 124+223 | For service |
| 21.10.91 | 483.003 | 123+224 | 123+223 | Reverts to correct formation |
| 31.10.91 | 483.004 | 124+223 | 124+224 | Reverts to correct formation |
| January | (483.009 | 129+229 | 129+224 | Flooding of depot on 04.01.94. Temporary |
| 1994 | (483.004 | 124+224 | | formation until 08.02.94 |
| 08.02.94 | 483.004 | | 124+224 | Reverts to correct formation |
| 08.02.94 | 483.009 | 129+224 | 129+229 | Reverts to correct formation |
| 10.02.94 | (483.003 | 123+223 | 123+225 | 223 defective |
| | (483.005 | 125+225 | 125+223 | 125 collision at Ryde Pier Head |
| 16.12.94 | 123+225 renumbered unit 483.003 (for service) | | | |
| 16.12.94 | 125+223 renumbered unit 483.005 (withdrawn) | | | 125 & 223 scrapped 24.04.00 |
| 16.05.95 | 483.001 | 121+221 | 121+225 | For service |
| 16.05.95 | 483.003 | 123+225 | 123+221 | Out of service stored at Ryde |
| 28.06.96 | 483.001 | 121+225 | 121+222 | Out of service – scrapped 24.04.00 |
| 28.06.96 | 483.002 | 122-222 | 122+225 | For service |

**APPENDIX 30 – New Livery Details**

| Unit | O/S | R.E.S. | Details |
|------|-----|--------|---------|
| 483.004 | 15.01.00 | 21.03.00 | All blue with Dinosaur décor – named "Terry" |
| 483.006 | 28.01.00 | 20.03.00 | All blue with Dinosaur décor – Named "T-Rex" |
| 483.002 | 21.02.00 | 20.04.00 | All blue with Dinosaur décor – Named "Raptor" |
| 483.009 | 10.03.00 | 17.05.00 | All blue with Dinosaur décor – Named "Bronti" |
| 483.008 | 25.03.00 | 24.07.00 | All blue with Dinosaur décor – Named "Iggy" |
| 483.007 | 12.05.00 | 27.01.03 | In original "Underground" red with cream window pillars |

**APPENDIX 31 – SUMMARY OF FLOODED UNITS – 10.10.00**

| Unit | R.E.S. | Details |
|------|--------|---------|
| 483.002 | 20.06.01 | |
| 483.004 | 13.10.00 | |
| 483.006 | 03.12.00 | |
| 483.007 | 27.01.03 | Formal 'launch' in LT livery 24.01.03, in passenger service 27.01.03 |
| 483.008 | – | Unaffected |
| 483.009 | – | Unaffected |

**APPENDIX 32 – TRIPCOCK MODIFICATIONS**

| Unit | Completed |
|------|-----------|
| 483.002 | 17.04.02 |
| 483.004 | 12.01.02 |
| 483.006 | 01.01.02 |
| 483.007 | 24.01.03 |
| 483.008 | 02.02.02 |
| 483.009 | 03.02.02 |

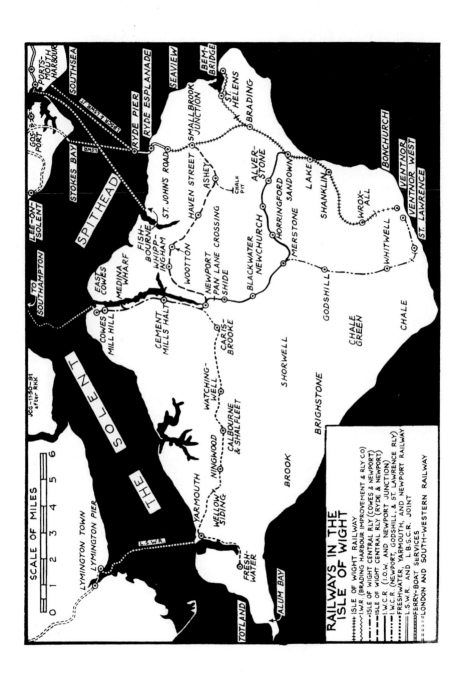

RAILWAYS IN THE
ISLE OF WIGHT

+++++++ ISLE OF WIGHT RAILWAY
ᴠᴠᴠᴠᴠᴠᴠ I.W.R. (BRADING IMPROVEMENT & RLY CO)
–·–·–·– ISLE OF WIGHT CENTRAL RLY (COWES & NEWPORT)
·········· ISLE OF WIGHT CENTRAL RLY (RYDE & NEWPORT)
·—·—·— I.W.C.R. (I.O.W. AND NEWPORT JUNCTION)
–––––– I.W.C.R. (NEWPORT, GODSHILL, & ST. LAWRENCE RLY)
•••••••• FRESHWATER, YARMOUTH, AND NEWPORT RAILWAY
○○○○○○ L.S.W.R. AND L.B.S.C.R. JOINT
ꞏꞏꞏꞏꞏꞏꞏꞏ FERRY-BOAT SERVICES
════════ LONDON AND SOUTH-WESTERN RAILWAY

SCALE OF MILES
0 1 2 3 4 5 6

XCG-1150-91
after RKK